FOREWORD BY STEPHEN FRY

THE EXTRAORDINARY
SONGS OF

CLIVE JAMES
PETE &ATKIN

LOOSE
CANON

IAN SHIRCORE

RedDoor

Published by RedDoor
www.reddoorpublishing.com

Every effort has been made to trace copyright holders and to obtain permission for the use of copyright material. The publisher apologises for any errors or omissions. If you believe you are the copyright owner of material used in this book and we have not requested your permission, please contact us so that we can correct any oversight.

The right of Ian Shircore to be identified as author of this Work has been asserted by him/her in accordance with sections 77 and 78 of the Copyright, Designs and Patents Act 1988

ISBN 978-1-910453-23-0

A CIP catalogue record for this book is available from the British Library

Cover design: Rawshock Design

Typesetting: www.typesetter.org

Printed in Great Britain by Bell and Bain Ltd, Glasgow

This one's for Zoë and Nick

Contents

Foreword by Stephen Fry

It's appallingly inconsiderate and unforgivably vain of me to have been secretly pleased all my life that Clive James and Pete Atkin never broke into the Big Time.

God knows, they deserved to. No-one British has written consistently better, sharper, sour-sweeter or more original and hauntingly memorable songs over so long and fruitful a partnership. Lennon and McCartney had just seven years of taking dictation from the muse. Atkin and James have spent half a century intermittently turning the ironically melancholic and the ruefully funny (or is it melancholically ironic and funnily rueful? All permutations of the four, I think) into an art form. Those of us who have hugged the secret of this wonderfully gifted pair to ourselves can't help feeling rather special and discerning, and we don't need anyone else to clutter up the premises of our small and select club. Val Doonican threatened to let the cat out of the bag when he recorded 'The Flowers and the Wine', ultimately with hilarious lack of consequences, as you can read within. And now, finally, the internet age has blown my selfish hopes out of the water. YouTube and the web can now satisfy all your Atkin-James needs, and a good thing too.

Way back when the world was young, a friend of mine lent me a cassette of *Beware of the Beautiful Stranger* and I instantly became what would be called today a fanboy. It was around this time that the Ella Fitzgerald songbooks were being reissued and lending class to the sound systems of every upmarket cafe, bistro and brasserie in the land. Our generation of sixth-formers and students felt that we were discovering Song, with a capital S, for the first time. There were lieder and there were pop songs, power ballads, disco and dance numbers, two-minute punk assaults and epic rock tracks that took the whole side of an LP to say nothing. But, in between, there had been, since the Jazz Age, Song (and, over the channel, *chanson*). What Lorenz Hart, Cole Porter and Irving Berlin perfected in the heyday of Tin Pan Alley, and Jacques Brel in postwar France, astonished me, and still does. But why had no-one British heard the call? Against all of Gershwin, Porter, Kern, Mercer and Rodgers, we might tentatively offer 'A Nightingale Sang in Berkeley Square' and 'These Foolish Things'. And against Trenet, Béart, Ferré and Brel, we can put up, in our defence, 'Where Do You Go To (My Lovely)?'. Classics all three, no question, but rare blooms in the most arid of British deserts.

Paul Hamlyn and EMI's good old MfP (Music for Pleasure) label, and those titans of Easy Listening, Mantovani, James Last and Bert Kaempfert, along with singers like Matt Monro, Engelbert Humperdinck, Shirley Bassey and Tom Jones, kept the songbook alive in Britain. And how cheesy they were considered by the hip. Processed cheese, at that. They were the Berni Inns of music, serving Babycham and prawn cocktails, rounded off with Irish coffee, while the rest of the world indulged in the sexy new fast-food revolution.

Now, of course, we look back and see that Shirley Bassey and Tom Jones rank alongside the great voices of the century. Listen to Shirley sing 'Climb Every Mountain'. She constructs a cathedral in your ears. Meanwhile folk went from briefly hot to terribly cold, without the intervening stage of cool. Worse than cheesy, it was goat's cheesy. Despite Ewan MacColl at the political end and Mike Harding at the comic, it rapidly became the mediocre stand-up's stale finger-in-ear-and-nasal-whine joke. Kate Rusby and others in the new Roots Music movement were to revivify the genre twenty-five years later, but all the creative energy of young Britain seemed to be being poured into pop and rock songs which made no real demand on the lyricist at all. If, like Austin Powers, you could say 'Yeah, baby!', you were in.

So where were the British songwriters to feed our undoubted orchestral and vocal talent, or the singer-songwriters to compare with Brel, Aznavour and Gainsbourg, or even with Dylan and Guthrie (Woody and Arlo)?

What I really wanted was not songs, but Song. Song is led by lyrics. Magnificent as the melodies of 'I Get a Kick Out Of You', 'Someone to Watch Over Me' and 'Let's Face the Music and Dance' undoubtedly are, more than half of what makes them great disappears when you hear an instrumental-only version.

So when I first listened to that tape of *Beware of the Beautiful Stranger* (was there ever such a title? No wonder I was immediately captivated), it was at just the right time. I was ready. Without knowing it, I had thirsted to hear British Song for a long time and hadn't really noticed that there wasn't any. 'Here is no water but only rock and roll', as TS Eliot didn't quite say.

Clive James, of course, was already well known to me from his own writing, from Monty Python's parodies of him and from his immortal

Observer television column. He remains the only great and creative critic of TV that has ever lived. And he's still at it – his new collection, *Play All*, a joyful analysis of the new indoor sport of binge watching, came close to making me actually wet myself. For much of my life, his crinkly grin and yo-yoing cadences were an essential part of British television, gifting us with an array of documentaries and his own brand of light chat in a big studio and heavy colloquy in a small one.

From the Seventies on, an avalanche of published criticism, poetry, commentary and memoir propelled him into the position of a cultural phenomenon: lunch in Notting Hill with Hitchens, Amis, Fenton and Rushdie, afternoon writing an essay on Rilke and a column about Sue Ellen from *Dallas*, then supper and a show with Margarita Pracatan and Princess Di. If dull old Henry hadn't got to the surname first, the word 'Jamesian' would be used today for Clive's kaleidoscopic, cock-eyed and cocky, playful and verbally incandescent, furiously well-read and stunningly well-informed high-, middle- and lowbrow practice.

But, of course, he is *clever*. And both his homeland and his adopted country have an issue with clever. They don't understand that intelligence is an emotion and that putting something well, extraordinary well, is not, in fact, cheating. Wit does not look down on the dirt of human experience, it penetrates it. Wit is not dishonest; it is quite dreadfully truthful. But the intellectual reach and formidable cerebral equipment of Clive James (*cf* Tom Stoppard and Jonathan Miller) have led people to suppose that he cannot *do* feelings, but only *play* with them like a cat with a mouse. Those perfect rhymes and gem-like internal bounces and rhythmic shifts surely betray too organised a mind for ordinary love, loss and living. If we are to believe that kind of claptrap, then a Hallmark greeting card is more honest than the sonnets of Donne, whereas, of course, the opposite is true. Sentiment and mush make us wince, not because they are cheap and easy (though they are) but because they lie to us.

Song itself, unlike poetry or 'songs', has to consist of *perfect* rhyming. Look at/listen to Sondheim and Porter. Half-rhymes, eye-rhymes and assonances won't do. Nor homophones. Clive revisited the song 'Faded Mansion on the Hill', from *Driving Through Mythical America*, where the word 'believe' had been, he decided, improperly paired with 'leave'. He changed it to 'retrieve', which, while semantically at great variance, turned out to work absurdly well in the song. Such technical faddishness as that re-tinkering might suggest a clinical or disengaged approach, and again the reverse is true. For, endlessly gifted verbal engineer that he is, he knows that only when the words are *right* will a song enter and animate the heart of the listener.

When you read his lyrics, you encounter a poet not of the clever, the chic or the self-possessed, but of the loser, the lonely and the lovelorn. He champions the hapless and the doubtful. I get images of Jacques Tati sitting in an Edward Hopper diner while British rain pelts down in the street outside. Funny, sad, beautiful, true. The pain and melancholia give the songs what wine connoisseurs call a long finish. They stay with you. But, of course, you shouldn't be reading the lyrics at all – not until you've first *heard* them, and not in Clive's voice, but in Pete's, and sung to his music.

Crammed with glorious brilliancies as Clive's lyrics are, they are in-finitely enhanced, enriched and ennobled by Pete's vocals, which are attractive, nimble, involving and always perfectly in tune (so much rarer than you might think, and always worth pointing out). The musical writing, which at first blush appears precise, neat, fitting, natural, wonderfully patterned, charming and tuneful, wraps around the words, just as the words wrap around the music, like Escher's drawing hands. It's exactly as 'musical' as it needs to be, without ever showing off. Which is such an achievement that it really is showing off. If using words like 'neat' and 'precise' sounds like damning with faint praise, whiz to the website or download the new recordings (*Midnight Voices* and *The Colours of the Night*) from the usual digital depots. You'll agree, I'm sure, that the neatness and precision in the mechanism of Pete's songwriting is every bit as emotionally engaging as the elegance, wordplay and dazzling internal rhymes and leaps and plunges of lyrical invention that it musicalises. And, when he wants to, he can rock the casbah, too, which no mere wordsmith can ever really manage.

Dorothy Parker described the musical comedy partnership of Wodehouse, Bolton and Kern as 'her favourite indoor sport'. That goes for me with Pete and Clive (to give them the conflated Cook and Moore billing that must irritate them excessively). Well, my favourite after darts and snooker, at any rate. This has been far too long and probably self-indulgent an introduction and I apologise. It's just that opportunities to ventilate my feelings about the Top Two don't come along very often. All I should have written as an introduction to this marvellous telling of their story are the words 'Thank' and 'You'.

Stephen Fry
Los Angeles
May 2016

1

Fifty Years in the Racket

At the time of writing, Clive James is Britain's best-known living poet. With the possible exception of Roger McGough, whose early fame was greatly helped by having a Number 1 hit single with a pop group that included Paul McCartney's brother, he is just about the only poet whose status as a household name spans every household in the country.

It's a level of recognition poets like Wendy Cope, Andrew Motion and even the wonderful Carol Ann Duffy can only dream of. But these people are singleminded. Poetry is what they do. Clive has never been remotely singleminded. His fame is based on a vast range of tirelessly productive creative activity. He has written serious poetry and bestselling memoirs, thoughtful literary criticism and a new translation of Dante to set alongside several decades of trenchant, informed and opinionated newspaper and radio journalism and a long string of hugely popular television chat shows and documentaries. By being everywhere, doing everything and refusing to pigeonhole his talents, he has become an inescapable part of our culture.

What he's not known for – beyond a small and passionate cult following – is his songwriting. The 200 or so songs co-written by Clive and his musical partner, Pete Atkin, are probably the least-known part of his creative output. And that's a shame, because this catalogue of wonders, built up over nearly half a century, includes some of his finest work.

Nobody loves a smart-arse, they told us. But it's not true. Some of us can't help being drawn to the flash and glitter of pyrotechnic wordplay, the knotted allusions and cross-references and exuberant technical ingenuity that show up in everything Clive writes, in poetry, prose or song. For us, it's about savouring the phrase, the idea, the image, the moment. Each stanza, paragraph or verse gives us something unexpected and unworn, thrown together with reckless energy in the laboratory of an extraordinary mind. When carping commentators accuse him of flaunting his erudition, dressing himself in false modesty and just plain showing off, the response surely has to be 'Yes, and…?' The man is unique, and he gives us unique pleasures, for which we are grateful.

When I first knew Pete and Clive, in the early 1970s, the songs were the thing. As each new album brought fresh and unpredictable joys – 'Touch Has a Memory' on *Beware of the Beautiful Stranger*, 'The Flowers and the Wine' on *Driving Through Mythical America*, 'Thirty Year Man' on *A King at Nightfall* and *The Road of Silk*'s 'Senior Citizens', to pick just an arbitrary few – I was convinced that the James/Atkin partnership was on its way to fame and fortune. I was not alone. I saw the reaction as audiences heard these songs for the first time and instantly took them to their hearts. And I became increasingly aware that the songs were gaining influential fans, such as John Peel and Kenny Everett, whose enthusiasm would surely help them reach a broader public.

2

In the early volumes of his *Unreliable Memoirs*, Clive mentions several times that he and Pete had a master plan. The way they saw it back then, the songs they were writing would be the gold mine that funded everything else they wanted to do in their lives. But for that to work, they would have to make a hit single of their own or, as seemed more likely at the time, produce songs that other, better-known artists would cover. That wouldn't make them household names, but it could potentially generate a stream of songwriting royalties.

The theory was sound. Singers like Julie Covington (a friend from Cambridge Footlights days, later to have an international No 1 with 'Don't Cry for Me Argentina') swooped on their work with delight. But it sometimes seemed that the wrong people got hold of the wrong songs. The one cover version that made any useful contribution to their finances came much later, in 1981, when the man with the cardigan and the rocking chair, Val Doonican, sang 'The Flowers and the Wine' on his *Quiet Moments* album. As Pete points out, ruefully, that one recording made rather more money than all six classic Atkin/James albums put together.

With the cruel clarity of hindsight, Clive commented later that the chief obstacle to achieving mass commercial success was him.

'My assumption that popular music could be dragged towards literature was fundamentally wrongheaded,' he declared, in *North Face of Soho*, the fourth volume of his memoirs. 'I was killing us with every clever lyric that I wrote.'

But back in the early, heady days, when live audiences were lapping up everything they had to offer and Pete was being asked back, time and again, for late-night sessions on John Peel's much-loved radio shows, no-one was complaining that the songs were too obscure. All we could see was that a new and original voice had appeared, singing material that combined powerful emotions, startling ideas and self-effacing humour with some great tunes. Surely that would be enough. Surely we would soon be able to stop saying 'You know, Clive James, the guy who writes the Observer TV column, the one who used to do that *Cinema* programme – he's a songwriter, too.'

We did, of course. We moved on to saying 'You know, Clive James, the guy on the telly – he's a songwriter, too.' And in later years we moved on even further. Everyone knew who Clive James was. Now all we had to say was 'You know, *the* Clive James.' With the success of *The Book of My Enemy* and the recent *Sentenced to Life*, Clive was even getting the recognition he had always wanted as a serious, though seldom solemn, poet. But the song lyrics have remained resolutely in the shadows. For Clive, and Pete, that has always been a disappointment. It's not like the comedian who yearns to play Hamlet, because Clive has been both the comic and the tragedian in his day, and won plaudits in both roles. It's just that he sees these songs as some of the most important work he's ever done.

'This is the work I'm known least for, but which is closest to my heart,' he said on the John Peel Show in 2000.

For thousands, but not millions, of us, these songs provide snatches of melody and fragments of lyrics that float in and out of our heads, unbidden, along with all the scraps of rock genius and pop gimmickry we carry through our daily lives in the jukebox of the brain.

They jostle with 'Life on Mars' and 'Wild Thing', 'Wonderwall' and '(Girl) Put Your Records On', 'Yakety Yak' and 'Sexual Healing', 'Common People' and 'Gangnam Style', 'Knowing Me, Knowing You' and 'Happy', clambering over each other in that dusty, unsorted attic of half-remembered hits and personal favourites. These songs are just as firmly planted, just as ineradicable, as any Top Ten single. We feel sorry for people who don't know them. We corner friends and force them to sit and listen, whether the moment's right or not. We bring them up in conversation ('Yes, like I said, *the* Clive James') and deplore the fact that nobody has re-released the re-releases of the 1970s albums.

We cheer out loud when celebrity fans like Stephen Fry, Charlie Brooker and historian Simon Schama and DJs like Stuart Maconie mention the Atkin/James albums and point their own fans towards them. And we wonder, as Clive James has been wondering for several decades, why his unique gift for engaging a mass following for his writing, TV shows and poetry has never quite stretched as far as winning a larger audience for the songs that he and Pete have written.

The unplanned career break from songwriting that occurred while Clive rose to international fame and Pete built a glittering career as a BBC Radio producer meant there was a gap a generation long between *Live Libel* (1975) and the duo's next album of newly-written songs, *Winter Spring* (2003). This was followed, in 2007, by *Midnight Voices*, effectively a greatest hits collection, though the triumphant reworkings of old favourites such as 'Master of the Revels', 'Thief in the Night' and 'The Hypertension Kid' were often very different from the original recordings. The latest, and last, album, *The Colours of the Night*, came in 2015 and included new delights like

'The Way You Are With Me' and 'The Closer Someone Is' which must surely rekindle the possibility of cover versions by other artists.

Even during the gap years, though, Clive's interest in exploring the possibilities of popular songwriting never left him. There were brief flirtations with the idea of writing with other artists, including Elvis Costello and Gerry Rafferty, but the magic wasn't there. Frustration reigned. Pete was the man who could bring out what was bubbling inside him, and it was only when they picked up where they'd left off and started writing together again that the juices started flowing.

'The only real cure for frustration is work, and for the quarter of a century we were behind the moon, I kept in shape by writing poems, which have their own music – or should have,' he told *Guardian* readers in 2008.

'But I always missed the thrill of hearing a set of syllables being absorbed by a row of notes, in a kind of mid-air mating dance that transmits a new emotion.'

When Clive James was presented with a special BAFTA award in 2015, the *Telegraph* rushed to celebrate this honour with an article listing thirty of his 'most memorable quotes'. Predictably, the journalists got it wrong. The list brought together some wonderful lines, from Clive's bluntly dismissive comment on George W Bush ('Delivering the State of the Union? That bloke couldn't deliver pizza') to his inspired response to Beyoncé's performance at Glastonbury: 'Beyoncé and pathos are strangers. Amy Winehouse and pathos are flatmates – and you should see the kitchen.' It included insights that were intended to be taken seriously ('Fiction is life with the dull bits left out') and his vivid description of veteran romantic novelist

Barbara Cartland: 'Twin miracles of mascara, her eyes looked like the corpses of two small crows that had crashed into a chalk cliff.' But it left out the one quote Clive is most likely to be remembered for.

When he described Arnold Schwarzenegger as looking like 'a brown condom full of walnuts', Clive James introduced a bizarrely graphic image and a new phrase into the English language. It has already hung around for thirty years on both sides of the Atlantic and Schwarzenegger, now well past pensionable age, is rumoured to be too scared to die for fear of seeing it quoted in every obituary ('Walnuts Condom Man Was Film Star and Governor'). The image is irresistible – brutally picturesque and poetically original. The fact that Leonardo da Vinci once wrote something similar about lesser artists painting limbs so stiff and graceless they looked like 'a bag of nuts' and 'more like a bundle of radishes than naked muscles' has nothing to do with it. Leonardo was not referring to Schwarzenegger. If he had been, I'm sure he'd have mentioned the condom as well. And if Clive was drawing on some vague memory of the Da Vinci image (he is, after all, a notorious student of Italian culture), that's probably more a matter of great Renaissance minds thinking alike than any direct reference to Leonardo's phrase.

Clive and Pete never quite got round to writing a song about the Terminator, so the condom full of walnuts does not appear in any of their lyrics. But many of their creations contain equally dazzling and unforgettable turns of phrase. Alongside Clive's inventive imagery and gleeful twisting of old ideas into new forms, it is one of the many delights in store for anyone meeting these extraordinary songs for the first time.

2

First Meeting

In the late Sixties and early Seventies, I was involved in running a folk music club in West London, in the low, vaulted crypt under a Catholic church on Richmond Hill. I didn't like folk music much – I was more interested in the Beatles and the Stones, Smokey Robinson and Marvin Gaye, Muddy Waters and Jimi Hendrix – and I hated the musty, fusty, dowdy atmosphere of many of the traditional folk clubs I visited.

But within weeks of opening, in March 1968, the Hanging Lamp Folk Club found itself standing on the threshold of a revolution, as a dazzling array of young and unrecognised musicians approached us in the hope of being booked. Apart from the main guest each Monday night, there would be room for five or six 'floor spots', in which people from the audience would come up and perform one or two songs. For some of these people, it was the first and only time they would sing or play in public – and it was often just as well. For others, the would-be professionals who were looking for bookings, it was the chance to show what they could do.

In the course of the next year or two, our little folk club became the *X Factor* of its day. We met Ralph McTell, loved his songs and his Blind Blake fingerpicking style and paid him £2 for his first gig at the Lamp. We found the 19-year-old John Martyn playing to a handful of people on a barge in Kingston and lured him to Richmond for the same princely fee. McTell had not yet written 'Streets of London' and Martyn's repertoire was an odd mix of whimsy and old blues numbers, though his spectacular, flamboyant playing stopped everyone in their tracks. We discovered Mike Oldfield, then 15, playing second fiddle (or, more accurately, backing guitar) to his older sister in a hippy-ish duo called The Sallyangie, and the legendary Welsh ragtime genius, John James, whose wonderful technique meant he often sounded as if he was playing two or three guitars at once. Even when we went for more traditional folk club fare, with the larger-than-life Irish comedian/folk singer Noel Murphy, who was married to my best friend, Heather, we found ourselves watching performances of extraordinary virtuosity.

Noel was no great shakes as a guitarist, but he had an eye for talent. He had been on tour in Fife and recruited Davey, a wonderful 17-year-old mandolin and banjo player, to work with him. I remember seeing this prodigy for the first time, squatting shyly on a stool next to Noel, hidden behind a cascade of pale blonde hair, as he tore into a traditional reel, played at a speed that made his fingers a blur. I was already gasping at the lad's effortless mastery of the mandolin when he flipped his hand from below the fretboard to above it, effectively playing the instrument backwards, and continued his solo with the same easy fluency. It was a moment of stunning bravura and show-manship, and I will never forget it. It came as no surprise when this youngster, Davey Johnstone, moved on from supporting Noel and took his career in other directions, adding the guitar to his arsenal and eventually becoming Elton John's lead guitarist and musical director for the next four decades.

Almost by accident, our little club began to build a reputation as the place to go to see the best guitarists and other instrumentalists in town.

But we were equally interested in finding and encouraging song-writers who could do something new and fresh with their lyrics. We repeatedly booked Al Stewart, who had shared a flat in Stepney with Paul Simon and whose experimental writing stretched as far as 'Love Chronicles', a winding 18-minute, 1200-word odyssey of adolescence, lust and romance. 'Love Chronicles' broke new ground when it used an unexpected rhyme for the word 'plucking', marking an emotional turning point as the narrator experiences something that's 'less like fucking' and more, he feels, like making love. It was the first time any of us had heard that word in a song and we thought it bold, modern and realistic. When Al recorded the *Love Chronicles* album, I was always worried that my mother might turn up while the song was playing, leaving me with the choice of cutting the track off halfway through ('And so on and so on. I won't bore you with the rest of it, Mum') or coughing very loudly after 'less like'.

We watched, over the months, as Ralph McTell's lyrics grew subtler and more distinctive and John Martyn gradually developed the easy way with words that eventually led to songs like 'May You Never' and 'Sweet Little Mystery'.

But you can't win them all, and our star-spotting antennae were not infallible. According to Elvis Costello's recent book, the Hanging

Lamp was the scene of his own first-ever public performance, a floor spot debut so energising that at least one eminent member of the audience, Ewan MacColl, the man who composed 'The First Time Ever I Saw Your Face', immediately fell fast asleep. Quite a few of the floor singers could do that to you. Costello played Lindisfarne's 'Winter Song', a poignant (55%) or dirge-like (45%) epic, depending on your point of view. But if the 15-year-old Declan MacManus was showing any signs of his future genius, they were lost on me that night. Indeed, it was only a few years ago that I learned that the boy from East Twickenham had walked over Richmond Bridge week after week to sit at the feet of John James, John Martyn and our other regulars.

The first time we ever felt bowled over by the sheer class and ingenuity of the words we were hearing was the night Pete Atkin turned up and asked to play a floor spot. The main artist was Ralph McTell, a good friend of ours and already a rising star, and the club was packed with nearly two hundred people.

Pete, as ever, was polite, even reticent. He'd do three songs, he said, if that was OK. The floor spot list was already full and I hesitated to squeeze him in, but he'd come a long way and his manner seemed very professional, so I took an executive decision and dumped a couple of our local regulars to give him ten minutes or so. I was lucky enough to be at the side of the stage as he launched into 'Beware of the Beautiful Stranger'. Within seconds, you could see that the audience was listening with rapt attention. I'd had no idea what to expect, but my immediate thought was 'This is as good as anything you hear on the radio. We've got to book this guy.'

As the twists and turns of the narrative unfolded and the sceptical funfair visitor found himself face to face with the beautiful stranger in the gypsy's crystal ball ('I'm the one you'll meet after the one you know now'), I knew this was something different. It was funny, with some great wisecracks and one-liners. But it also carried an undertow of sadness (' "You live in a dream, and the dream is a cage," said the girl, "and the bars nestle closer with age" '). The song was a finely-crafted five-minute tragicomedy and I loved it. So did the audience, crammed in and squinting around the pillars of the whitewashed, orange-lit crypt. I can't remember what else Pete played. But it didn't matter. We were going to get him back.

When he came off stage and we broke for the interval (plastic beakers of tepid tea, coffee or sticky orange juice – no alcohol beneath St Elizabeth's church), I went into the hall that served as the dressing room to talk to Pete. He wasn't famous, so I was sure we'd be able to agree a suitably modest fee. But when I caught up with him, I was surprised to see that such an unknown performer had felt it necessary to bring a bodyguard with him. The man, chunky, heavyset, with small, dangerous-looking eyes, hovered at Pete's shoulder wherever he went, wearing an incongruous flowered shirt that only emphasised his bouncer's bulk. I felt awkward. We weren't used to singers who brought their own security people along.

In retrospect, I realise that I must have been one of the last people in this country to meet Clive for the first time without having some idea who he was. Over the next few years, his increasingly frequent television appearances made his face one of the most recognisable in Britain. As he moved from print journalism into the nation's sitting rooms, Clive James became public property. He became known as a TV critic and commentator, a satirical poet and a provocative columnist, polarising opinions and attracting lavish praise and energetic sniping from all directions. Everyone knew Clive James, and everyone had strong opinions about his work, his wit, his voice and even his hairline. Yet his songs managed to remain largely unknown. His collaboration with Pete has lasted nearly fifty years, but the cult following it has won them has always stubbornly refused to turn into a mass audience.

That night, at the folk club, we soon got over the confusion about Clive's role. Though Pete was the front man, the performer who took their work up on stage and offered it to the world, it was his bouncer who did most of the talking. There was an album on the way, Clive told me, and they were writing songs at a rate that would soon provide enough material for two or three more. We talked about Dylan and Joni Mitchell and Lennon and McCartney and Leiber and Stoller's hits, from 'Hound Dog' and 'Jailhouse Rock' to 'I (Who Have Nothing)' and 'Stand By Me'. We talked about Cole Porter and the Gershwins and Shakespeare. We talked (or he did) about Dante and Verlaine, who was already featured in one of their most popular songs, 'Girl on the Train'. I should have known I was out of my depth. By the time we got round to talking about money, I was convinced that we were potentially in at the start of something wonderful. I'd made up my mind. I was prepared to go to almost any lengths to make sure we were able to bring our audience a full evening of these unknown treasures.

'Would £15 be OK?' I asked.

3

Mistaken Identities

The big cliché about the Clive James/Pete Atkin creations, over the years, has always been that they were unclassifiable. Record shops didn't know where to display the LPs (though Clive suggested, helpfully, that the obvious category would be 'Difficult Listening') and radio stations couldn't quite see where these songs – romantic, witty, wordy, allusive, introspective, often humorous and frequently all these things at once – fitted into their programming.

In the clubs and colleges of the early 1970s, though, where un-suspecting audiences found themselves face to face with Pete's engaging, understated performances for the first time, categorisation was not a problem. People listened, liked what they heard and wanted more. By the time the first album, *Beware of the Beautiful Stranger*, came out, in 1970, there were already enough instantly memorable numbers to excite even first-time listeners. Songs like the title track, 'Have You Got a Biro I Can Borrow?' and 'Touch Has a Memory' may not have revealed all their depth and quality at first hearing, but they had an immediate appeal.

One of my early favourites, live and on the record, was 'All I Ever Did'. This delicate miniature seemed to me to show them at their best. There was nothing pretentious or overwrought about the lyrics, no obvious verbal fireworks or obscure references. Just a brief, well-crafted song, less than one minute long, about the end of an affair, with a simple, poignant melody and an unusual structure that left you wanting more.

Of course, the impression of simplicity was an illusion. Even the first two lines bear the trademark James/Atkin twist, the subtle undermining of expectations. 'All I ever did while you were here was done for you,' sings Pete. The classic protestation of the rejected lover. 'Or so I said, perhaps through fear that nothing less would make you stay.' Hmmmm. That muddies the waters with a dash of realism. But before there's time to reconcile the impressions created by these two lines, we are carried through to what is clearly a sincere tribute to the impact of this love. 'All I'd ever done or ever was meant something new / Or so I thought, perhaps because the past seemed night and this seemed day.'

There's hardly a word of more than one syllable and the tune is deceptively straightforward, though the fact that the song moves through eight different chords in 57 seconds hints that there's a little more going on than meets the eye. I liked its brevity and the unusual verse – chorus – coda structure, repeating only the first line-and-a-half of the verse pattern and then bringing proceedings abruptly to a close with the song's shortest line, 'All you ever said was "Goodbye".'

Few compositions, then or now, err in the direction of being too short. I felt that 'All I Ever Did' took a risk by being so compact, and got away with it, triumphantly, by the simple trick of saying what it had to say and then stopping. I liked that. It implied a sense of form

15

and discipline that only added to my conviction that Clive and Pete were destined for great things. I liked what they'd done already, and I felt sure they would go on to write the kind of songs that would emerge as much-covered standards. They might not be the new George and Ira Gershwin – who ever could be? – but they would go far. In 'All I Ever Did', I thought, they had shown the ability to blend words and music in something close to perfection.

Besides running our folk club in Richmond, I was writing music reviews for London's hippest magazine, *Time Out*, and several other publications at the time. I took the opportunity, everywhere I could, to draw attention to the quality of songs like this and 'Have You Got a Biro I Can Borrow?', extolling the virtues of Clive's extraordinary and unpredictable lyrics and Pete's inspired musical settings.

But in the case of 'All I Ever Did', I'd got it all wrong. Of all the examples I could have chosen to illustrate the power of their combined talents, this was the least appropriate.

It took me some forty years to notice it, but the credits for this brilliant little song read 'Words and music by Pete Atkin'. Almost uniquely, this was a solo effort by Pete. Apart from the crowd-pleasing helter-skelter lyrics he wrote for Meade Lux Lewis's 'Honky Tonk Train Blues', this was just about the only time Pete got a chance to show what he could do with the words.

In my defence, though, the Clive and Pete partnership had already been operating for several years by this time and it's not unreasonable to suggest that they had probably grown together and influenced each other in the course of writing a catalogue that already added up to nearly a hundred songs. Though this delightful little masterpiece is Pete's alone, I still believe you can hear Clive's voice in there somewhere.

Talking to Pete about 'All I Ever Did' recently, I discovered that he had always felt he was doing something with this short song that had not really been possible before. Although the 33rpm vinyl long player had been generally available since the early 1950s, almost every album of the time was made up of a collection of three-minute tracks. Though each side of an LP could be up to 20, or even 25, minutes long, the idea of taking advantage of this new technology and writing and recording songs or sequences that were much longer than three minutes was something that had not been explored. Radio stations built their programming around three-minute slots, and nobody wanted to put out recordings that would automatically be excluded from the airwaves.

In the middle to late Sixties, led, in this, as in everything else, by Dylan and the Beatles, the music industry had started to realise that a song could be as long as it needed to be. When Dylan included a seven-minute track, 'Chimes of Freedom', on his 1964 album, *Another Side of Bob Dylan*, the revolution had begun. On his next LP, he did it again, with 'It's Alright Ma (I'm Only Bleeding)' running to 7 minutes 10 seconds. 'Desolation Row', on 1965's *Highway 61 Revisited*, made that look lightweight, checking in at 11'20". In 1966, Dylan made the rock world's first double album, *Blonde on Blonde*, featuring 'Sad Eyed Lady of the Lowlands', which beat even that by a second or two. The song took up the whole of Side Four of the double album.

When the Beatles chose to string together a 16-minute eight-song medley on *Abbey Road*, the last album they made, the format-busting moved to a new phase. But still there were very few ultra-short songs.

'The immediate inspiration, for "All I Ever Did", in terms of format, was a song called "Once Was a Time I Thought", which formed the last track on the second album by the Mamas & the Papas,' Pete told me.

The song, a quirky semi-tongue-twister arranged for four virtually unaccompanied voices, lasted just 58 seconds. Its startling brevity appealed to Pete, and seemed to open new doors.

'Aha, I thought. The brakes are off. From now on, a song really can be as long or as short as its content dictates. Wouldn't it be interesting to try to write something that was neat and complete and less than a minute long, without the pressure to fill it out with extra verses or repeating choruses?'

Clive and Pete had always been clear that one of the main differences between a poem and a song was the need for immediacy. A poem is entitled to demand a careful reading, followed by re-reading to tease out its subtleties. A song has to work first time, in real time. Even in their most complex compositions, songs like 'Driving Through Mythical America' and 'Screen-Freak' where Clive's lyrics were at their most dense and allusive, they knew they needed to create an immediate connection with the audience. A poem would remain on the page, inviting further investigation and enjoyment. A song would be performed once and would then be gone into the night. If it didn't work straight away in a live performance, it would not be doing its job.

'All I Ever Did' illustrates this perfectly. Every time Pete sings it, there is a brief moment of startled silence after the final 'Goodbye', as the audience adjusts quickly to the fact that that's it. The song is over. It has said what it had to say and stopped, just exactly the way songs never do. I don't know of another example that does the same thing and achieves the same dramatic effect. But I do know that audiences love the feeling of being gently wrongfooted by the sudden ending to this deceptively simple-seeming masterpiece.

All I Ever Did

WORDS AND MUSIC BY PETE ATKIN

All I ever did while you were here was done for you,
Or so I said, perhaps through fear
That nothing less would make you stay

All I'd ever done or ever was meant something new,
Or so I thought, perhaps because
The past seemed night and this seemed day

All I'd ever seen was black and white,
All I'd ever sung was off-key.
All I'd ever spoken sounded trite.
And then with you I was all the things I wished to be

All I ever did while you were here was done for you.
Now through my tears I'm asking why
All you ever said was 'Goodbye'

4

Beware of the Beautiful Stranger

The title track of the first Pete Atkin album was one of the first songs Clive and Pete wrote together. They were in Cambridge, working on material for a Footlights show, when Clive handed Pete two sheets of paper with the typed lyrics of 'Beware of the Beautiful Stranger'.

'It really was early days for us,' Pete says. 'We'd written maybe a dozen songs together at that point. I didn't think: "Wow, that's great lyric writing." I just thought: "Oh good. It's another song for me to work on." And I knew I'd have to be a bit careful. The rhythm of the words was ideal for storytelling, but the song was long – over 500 words, with ten identical six-line verses – and I could see that repetition might be a problem. I didn't want to fall into the trap of just writing a boring version of some old folk tune, because that wouldn't carry it. At the same time, I didn't want to write anything that would dominate and distract from the lyrics.'

Some songs are worth waiting for, though. Unlike Elton John, who is rumoured to look at a new set of words from Bernie Taupin or whoever he is writing with, give it half an hour and then discard it if the music has not come to him more or less straight away, Pete was prepared to take his time.

'It was several days before I came up with the idea. As always, getting the tempo and rhythm right was the first step. I can't make a song work till I've done that. Then I came up with that simple, long, descending melody line, probably influenced, I think, by the opening of the Beach Boys' 'Heroes and Villains'. And then I had to find some way of coming to terms with the sheer length of the song. I needed a way to break it up a little, without being self-consciously quirky.'

The key to this turned out to be to introduce a bit of musical space into the two middle lines of each stanza, stemming the torrent of words to provide a change of pace and a two-bar burst of strummed guitar. These end up being double-length lines, taking twice as long as the lines before and after.

'It seemed to work – and it seemed to work well in every verse, helping the pacing of the story. I still think it does. The glory is all Clive's, because it's the story and the jokes and the overall brilliance of the lyric that make the song. But I did my bit, and I'm proud of that.'

'Beware of the Beautiful Stranger' is a five-act tragicomedy, with three speaking parts (the Man, the Gypsy and the Beautiful Stranger – each with a distinctly different way of using words) plus a narrator. It's effectively science fiction, driven by the advanced technology of the crystal ball. And like all good science fiction, from HG Wells and John Wyndham onwards, it begins with the everyday. The Man, unbelieving and probably bored with his visit to the fairground, wanders into the Gypsy's caravan, hands over a pound and is told, in the routine phrase, to 'Beware of the Beautiful Stranger.'

Pretending to go along with the joke that the Gypsy can see into the future, the Man points out that he's already got a problem with his own Beautiful Stranger. The Gypsy, though, starts to get serious and warns that the Beautiful Stranger will 'utterly screw up your life' and 'tempt you from home, from your children and wife'. The Man assumes this is just smart guesswork and retorts 'The future you see there has all come about.' But he's interested, and hands over some more money.

'Does it show you the girl, as she happens to be?' he asks. Or is it, 'Does it show you the girl, as she happens to be, a Venus made flesh in a shell full of sea?'? The ambiguity derives from the Janus-like syntax, which manages to face two ways at once. One way, the Man is stating that his own problematical Stranger is, as it happens, a woman rather than a man. The other way round he's asserting that she is a Botticellian beauty, with extraordinarily long hair, a big scallop shell and no clothes.

'Hmmm. I've never thought of that,' says Pete. 'I don't consciously sing the comma, but the line is ambiguous.'

Either way, the Man is intrigued, though still largely unbelieving. 'Does it show you the shape of my danger?' he taunts the Gypsy. 'Can you show me the Beautiful Stranger?'

So far, everything in the song has been essentially naturalistic. There is a pause, for one verse, while the Gypsy negotiates more cash ('Slip me your wallet, sit tight and believe') and then a dramatic and unexpected revelation. The technology does work. The crystal ball does show the future. The Man watches as an image forms in the glass, but it's not who he's expecting. Instead, the Beautiful Stranger turns out to be just that, 'a total and beautiful stranger'.

As she speaks for the first time ('Hello there,' she said, with her hand to her brow. 'I'm the one you'll meet after the one you know now'), the song lifts off into the unexplored territory of the imagination.

'There's no room inside here to show you us all, but behind me the queue stretches right down the hall,' she says, matter-of-factly. 'For the damned, there is always a stranger. There is always a Beautiful Stranger.'

Another dramatic pause, as the Gypsy does her 'That's your lot… One last word' routine. Then it's on to some of the finest and most chilling lines ever to make their way into what could be mistaken for a light comic song.

'You live in a dream and the dream is a cage,' says the girl, 'And the bars nestle closer with age.' Now she's loading the ambiguities on, too. Those bars? Are they the bars of the cage? Or is this also a hint that alcohol may become a bigger factor in the Man's life as he ages? 'Your shadow burned white by invisible fire, you will learn how it rankles to die of desire, as you long for the Beautiful Stranger,' says the Beautiful Stranger, vanishing abruptly before any questions can be asked.

As the Gypsy returns his now-empty wallet, the Man is left stunned, perhaps wondering whether this whole Skype call from the future has been some projection of his own suggestible imagination. But the Gypsy has seen and heard everything that's happened, as she confirms with the last line of the song: 'Give my love to the Beautiful Stranger.' She believes, and he is forced to believe, too.

This is a five-and-a-half minute epic – smart, funny, knowing, startlingly original and, in its own way, uniquely satisfying. People hearing it for the first time laugh in all the right places and clap with delight at the end. Others, the long-term Pete Atkin fans who have heard it dozens of times before, still enjoy it, though they may laugh in less obvious places.

'The song worked then and it still works now,' says Pete, 'It's an amazing song, a fascinating piece of work. And it's all because of the apparently effortless magic of the writing. It's all about Clive's skill, the pacing and the way he tells the story, though I think what I did with the music certainly helped. He just keeps on coming up with the stuff, with surprises in every verse and at every turn. It's long, of course, and it probably goes on longer than it reasonably should, but when you get to the end, you don't want it to stop. Clive always seems to undervalue it a bit, but I think it's a fantastic lyrical achievement.'

Beware of the Beautiful Stranger

WORDS BY CLIVE JAMES, MUSIC BY PETE ATKIN

On the midsummer fairground alive with the sound
And the lights of the Wurlitzer merry-go-round,
The midway was crowded and I was the man
Who coughed up a quid in the dark caravan
To the gypsy who warned him of danger:
'Beware of the Beautiful Stranger'

'You got that for nothing,' I said with a sigh
As the queen's head went up to her critical eye.
'The lady in question is known to me now.
And I'd like to beware, but the problem is how?
Do you think I was born in a manger?
I'm in love with the Beautiful Stranger'

The gypsy (called Lee, as all soothsayers are)
Bent low to her globular fragment of star.
'This woman will utterly screw up your life.
She will tempt you from home, from your children and wife.
She's a devil and nothing will change her.
Get away from the Beautiful Stranger.'

'That ball needs a re-gun,' I said, shelling out.
'The future you see there has all come about.
Does it show you the girl, as she happens to be,
A Venus made flesh in a shell full of sea?
Does it show you the shape of my danger?
Can you show me the Beautiful Stranger?'

'I don't run a cinema here, little man,
But lean over close and tune in if you can.
You breathe on the glass, give a rub with your sleeve,
Slip me your wallet, sit tight and believe,
And the powers that be will arrange a
Pre-release of the Beautiful Stranger.'

In the heart of the glass, I saw galaxies born,
The eye of the storm and the light of the dawn.
And then, with a click, came a form and a face
That stunned me, not only through candour and grace,
But because she was really a stranger –
A total and beautiful stranger

'Hello there,' she said, with her hand to her brow.
'I'm the one you'll meet after the one you know now.
There's no room inside here to show you us all,
But behind me the queue stretches right down the hall.
For the damned, there is always a stranger.
There is always a Beautiful Stranger'

'That's your lot,' said Miss Lee, as she turned on the light.
'These earrings are hell and I'm through for the night.
If they'd put up a booster not far from this pitch
I could screen you your life to the very last twitch,
But I can't even get *The Lone Ranger*.
One last word from the Beautiful Stranger.'

'You live in a dream and the dream is a cage,'
Said the girl, 'And the bars nestle closer with age.
Your shadow burned white by invisible fire,
You will learn how it rankles to die of desire
As you long for the Beautiful Stranger,'
Said the vanishing Beautiful Stranger

'Here's a wallet for you and five nicker for me,'
Said the gypsy, 'And also here's something for free.
Watch your step on my foldaway stairs getting down,
And go slow on the flyover back into town.
There's a slight but considerable danger.
Give my love to the Beautiful Stranger.'

5

Learning from the
Great American Songbook

Irving Berlin, of course, was the daddy of them all, the pioneer who created the tradition of beautifully-crafted popular songs that Clive and Pete took as their inspiration. He was a freak, an oddball talent who couldn't read music and could only play the piano in one key, F sharp, so that everything he wrote was written almost entirely on the black notes. He got round this by using a transposing piano, with a lever underneath the keyboard that mechanically shifted the keys right or left, relative to the strings. He called it his 'trick piano'. But he had the ear and the imagination, and he employed a succession of musical secretaries to take down his tunes and sometimes supply suitable chords and harmonies. The young George Gershwin applied for this job once, but Berlin turned him down after hearing him play some of his own songs. 'What the hell do you want to work for anyone else for?' he asked.

Berlin wrote more than 1,200 songs, including 25 No 1 hits. He would start work after dinner and go on until 5am, often writing four songs in a night, with extra felt padding on the hammers of his piano and feathers stuffed inside the instrument to damp down the noise and avoid upsetting the neighbours in his apartment block. He prided himself on having written more bad songs than anyone else in the business. 'I've written more songs than anyone, so I guess I've written more bad songs, too,' he said. Many of the lesser creations were substantial hits at the time, though songs like 'Yiddle on Your Fiddle Play Some Rag Time' and 'Snookey Ookums' have been mercifully forgotten. What's left is a huge corpus of classics, including 'Alexander's Ragtime Band', 'God Bless America', 'White Christmas', 'Putting on the Ritz', 'You Can't Get a Man with a Gun' and 'I've Got My Love to Keep Me Warm'.

What's remarkable about this vast assortment of hits is its sheer variety. The ideas and lyrics range from the trite and maudlin to the sharp, the jokey, the ironic and the tragic. The tunes are quirky or magnificent, often structurally inventive and melodically playful. It's as if Irving Berlin had access to a universe of unwritten songs and simply plucked them from the ether as they flew past. He made it look so easy. And this apparent effortlessness, the art that conceals art, became the hallmark of the great American songwriting tradition that had its first flowering after the Great War.

It's there in George Gershwin, whose exuberant piano performances underline his sheer delight in his own musical genius. It's there in the hundreds of finely polished songs Richard Rodgers wrote with Lorenz Hart and Oscar Hammerstein. It's there, too, in Cole Porter's vast catalogue of hits, though history has tended to skate over the fact that he also wrote many lame and unsuccessful songs for shows that proved to be complete turkeys and were heavily panned by the critics. Half of Porter's career was made up of comebacks. The other half gave us 'Night and Day', 'You're the Top', 'Every Time We Say Goodbye', 'Anything Goes' and 'Who Wants to be a Millionaire?', but the point is that this pampered rich kid had to work at it, despite the casual gloss of the finished songs.

For Clive and Pete, the sense of awe created by these master craftsmen (and women – Pete has a particular soft spot for Dorothy Fields, whose collaborations with Jimmy McHugh and Jerome Kern gave us 'Sunny Side of the Street', 'The Way You Look Tonight' and 'Pick Yourself Up') was matched by a curiosity about how the magic was conjured up. Separately and together, they analysed these great songs, pulling them apart, trying to work out just what made them so exceptional. There were plenty of tips to pick up and lessons to learn, but one insight stood out above everything else. Whatever the subject matter, whatever the genre, however ingenious the rhyme scheme or glorious the melody, it was always the fit that mattered, the way the song came together as a whole.

'We realised that what all good songs have in common is the way the words and the music lock together, so that you can't separate them,' says Pete. 'You can't see the lyrics of "I've Got You Under My Skin" without thinking of the tune. It's impossible. And you can't hear the tune without immediately thinking of those words.

'As far as I can see, that applies across every genre and every type of popular song. It doesn't change. It's what links Irving Berlin and Cole Porter down the ages to Lennon/McCartney or Dylan or Elvis Costello or even the Arctic Monkeys.'

Both Clive and Pete had an intimate knowledge of the classic songs of the first half of the 20th century, though Clive, who already thought of himself as something of an expert, was astonished to discover, when they first got together, just how deep and wide Pete's range was.

'Atkin knew everything,' he wrote, more than thirty years later. 'He was particularly erudite on Tin Pan Alley. He knew Rodgers and Hart word for word and note for note. The same Mercer and Arlen songs that were my touchstones he could play and sing straight through from memory.'

Johnny Mercer and Harold Arlen created hits together with songs like 'Blues in the Night', 'Ac-Cent-Tchu-Ate the Positive' and 'One for My Baby (And One More for the Road)' and Clive had always loved Mercer's easy way with words.

Mercer's first taste of success had come in 1933, when he and Hoagy Carmichael, both exiled Southerners in New York, got together to write 'Lazybones'. Other Tin Pan Alley collaborations led to 'Hooray for Hollywood', 'Jeepers Creepers' and 'Fools Rush In'. But something special happened in the 1940s when Mercer and Harold Arlen starting writing together.

Arlen had worked successfully with other lyricists before teaming up with Johnny Mercer. He'd written hits like 'Stormy Weather' and 'Get Happy' with Ted Koehler, moving on to team up with Yip Harburg for 'Somewhere Over the Rainbow' and 'Paper Moon'. Both Mercer and Arlen were already respected and well established, but they immediately recognised that their collaboration would give them new scope to stretch their talents. Over the next few years, they wrote a string of songs that captured a characteristically con-versational tone that Clive found irresistible.

Johnny Mercer's 'One for My Baby' was the song Clive had always said 'sets my standard for the way a colloquial phrase can be multiplied in its energy by how it sits on a row of musical notes'. So it was a very special day when the aspiring lyricist met the ageing master in front of the cameras for the very first celebrity interview of his budding television career. But the result was an unmitigated disaster. The way Clive tells the story, he was so keen to make a success of it that he came into the interview over-prepared, showing off his knowledge of Mercer's career by making the classic beginner's mistake of including the answer in the question, over and over again, leaving the bemused guest with no opportunity to say much more than yes or no. When Mercer had gone, the producer delivered the bad news. 'We can't use this,' he said, and the interview was binned. It was a valuable lesson in TV technique, but a humbling experience for Clive, who was as anxious to impress his songwriting idol as he was to make a success of the interview.

Pete's view of the Johnny Mercer/Harold Arlen partnership was focused on the pair's ability to handle unconventional structures and verse forms and make them seem easy and natural. Arlen had written the music first for 'One For My Baby', presenting his lyricist with a potential hospital pass, as the tune meandered through a verse that was far longer than the conventional 32-bar Tin Pan Alley song. He knew that would create problems for his partner, but he also knew that Mercer was up to the challenge. From this unpromising beginning – Arlen called it 'a wandering song' and 'a tapeworm' – the duo managed to forge one of the finest examples of their craft.

'Johnny took it and wrote it exactly the way it fell. Not only is it long, but it also changes key. Johnny made it work,' said Arlen. 'I don't care what you give him, he'll find a way to save it, to help you.'

Throughout the Clive James/Pete Atkin partnership, the boot was usually on the other foot, as the words – or at least some of them – often tended to come together first. Clive would get the idea and Pete would receive a sheet or two of paper with neatly typed lyrics in all sorts of unlikely verse forms and rhyme schemes. Or, as in the case of 'An Empty Table', he would be handed an irregular, impressionistic cluster of lines and images – more like the outline for a short film than a set of lyrics – and invited to see what he could make of it. 'I don't know if this is a song or not,' Clive would say, and it would be up to Pete to decide whether it could be made to work.

Occasionally, however, the music did come first. Pete has always kept notebooks of ideas, phrases and snatches of melody that he could raid and cannibalise for new compositions. These fragments would sometimes hang around for years, waiting patiently to join up with other half-formed bits and pieces and turn into the music for a song.

'It was like an artist's sketchbook,' he says. 'These jottings hardly ever amounted to anything like a proper tune. They'd need another idea – maybe several other ideas – to turn them into something we could use.

'But it's not easy, whichever way round you approach it. There are no tricks, no secrets. You have to find your own answers to the problems of each particular song, and hope that the result seems inevitable and effortless.'

Ideally, of course, the composer is hoping that everything falls neatly into place first time round. And once in a while, it does.

'Sometimes it was straightforward,' Pete says. 'There are songs of ours where the music took no more than half an hour to write. But there are others that took me months and months, and went through all kinds of changes, even if they ended up sounding quite simple. I've still got a file of unfinished songs, and the reason they're unfinished is because the language is just too dense, not conversational enough. The lyrics sit there on the page and I can't find any way to stop them being poems and turn them into the sort of songs that will work, first time, for an audience that's never heard them before.'

At the other extreme from the over-dense lyrics that couldn't be brought to life, there are lightweight, crowd-pleasing romps that are all about jokes and wordplay and the ingenious fitting-together of unlikely rhymes and rhythms. One early live favourite, 'The Wristwatch for a Drummer', showed up a couple of years later on *A King at Nightfall.* This song is slight, in the extreme, but it's still a remarkable example of sheer playful exuberance and delight in the techniques of songmaking. The original joke, a cod advertising commercial for the Omega Incabloc Oyster Accutron '72, a specialist timepiece with a number of imaginative extras for hardworking percussionists, has not worn particularly well. But the words are simply amazing. Like Gershwin's "S Wonderful' (which coolly rhymes 'four-leaf clover time' with 'working overtime') or Porter's 'You're the Top' (where 'Strauss' is paired with 'mouse' and 'the National Gallery' with 'Garbo's salary'), it leaves you dazzled and gasping with pleasure at the outrageous effrontery of it all. There is one verse in which Clive reels off six successive rhymes ('free-form playing', 'overstaying', 'with the paying', 'deep decaying', 'stained and fraying', 'stooped and greying') and four successive uses of enjambement – rolling the meaning on to the beginning of the next line – just for the hell of it, just because he can.

> The Omega Incabloc Oyster Accutron '72
> Has a warning bell for free-form playing
> That tells you when you're overstaying
> Your tentative welcome with the paying
> Customers in the deep decaying
> Cellar club with the stained and fraying
> Velvet drapes and the stooped and greying
> Owner

It's not all like this, and the key rhyme ('drummer' and 'bummer') has rather lost its charm as fashions in musical slang have changed. But the song throws up several wonderfully atmospheric moments. 'So any time the brushes shimmer / On skins and brass, while the solo tenor / Slowly blows the lazy phrases…' is almost magical in its evocation of the hissy percussion (emphasised by the sibilant S's and Sh's) and the languid tenor sax (conjured up by the assonant O's, the liquid L's and the voiced Z sounds). That's real craftsmanship at work. Effects like that don't happen by accident. And there are some quietly gorgeous phrases, lurking amid the hubbub. We catch 'the golden glimmer of the wristwatch in the gloom' and the music is flown to us 'on plushly hushed extended wings'.

No-one in their right mind would claim that 'The Wristwatch for a Drummer' is a major song. It's a fun piece, almost a throwaway, a riotous ragbag of good gags and cheap shots (though I do still enjoy the simple pleasures of a joke like 'Elvin Jones has two and Buddy Rich wears three, / One on the right wrist, one on the left / And the third one around his knee').

What it does illustrate is the way both Clive and Pete had taken on board so many of the lessons and techniques to be found in the Great American Songbook, and their readiness, even at this early stage of their long songwriting career, to hurl them at the project in hand with nonchalant abandon and a great deal of skill.

The Wristwatch for a Drummer

WORDS BY CLIVE JAMES, MUSIC BY PETE ATKIN

The Omega Incabloc Oyster Accutron '72
Is the only wristwatch for a drummer.
It tells true, and it ain't no bummer

The Omega Incabloc Oyster Accutron '72
Can stand for more than mere immersion.
It thrives on whiplash, lurch and shock,
Trad, mainstream, bop and rock.
Baby Dodds had an early version

The Omega Incabloc Oyster Accutron '72,
Man, what a creation!
It's a mine of information.
A vernier scale, the date in Braille,

Sidereal time, the rate of crime

And the growth of population

It's got more jewels than Princess Grace.

Buckminster Fuller designed the case.

Leonardo engraved the face

And did the calibration.

And those knobs and screws and toggles…

The imagination boggles

The Omega Incabloc Oyster Accutron '72.

Without this timepiece there'd have been

No modern jazz to begin with.

Bird and Diz were tricky men for a drummer to sit in with.

Max Roach still wears the watch he wore when bop was new.

Elvin Jones has two and Buddy Rich wears three,

One on the right wrist, one on the left

And the third one around his knee

The Omega Incabloc Oyster Accutron '72

Has a warning bell for free-form playing

That tells you when you're overstaying

Your tentative welcome with the paying

Customers in the deep decaying

Cellar club with the stained and fraying

Velvet drapes and the stooped and greying

Owner

It'll count the bars and tell you when
The basset horn's coming in again.
It'll see you right while you're trading twelves
With a synthesizer played by elves.
Wear this watch and you'll keep in step
With Ornette Coleman and Archie Shepp.
Why be a loner?

Get the Omega Incabloc Oyster Accutron '72.
It's the only wristwatch for a drummer.
It tells true, and it ain't no bummer

So any time the brushes shimmer
On skins and brass, while the solo tenor
Slowly blows the lazy phrases,
You'll catch the golden glimmer
Of the wristwatch in the gloom.
So softly now let's sing its praises

For the music in the room,
Both beautiful and true,
On plushly hushed extended wings
Is flown to me and you

By the Omega Incabloc Oyster Accutron '72,
The only wristwatch for a drummer.
It tells true and it ain't no bummer

6

Period Piece

For those of us who still can't quite get our heads round the idea that half a century has passed since we were the young lords of the earth, enchanted by 'My Generation' and singing 'Hope I die before I get old' very loudly to annoy our parents, there are certain truths that have to be faced. We are actually, er, not young any more. Not as young as we were, anyway. And while we are naturally untouched by the taint of time, the world around us has changed and changed and changed again, so that what still seems like normality to us is now history.

It turns out we lived our early lives in a period, which we didn't realise at the time. You can tell that it's true, though, because anything you see on television that's set in the Sixties or Seventies is now a period piece, a studied recreation of a bygone age, usually marred by one or two glaring anachronisms that the hardworking researchers failed to recognise. I bet Jane Austen looks down and sniggers at every adaptation of *Pride and Prejudice* we ever see, for much the same reason.

From this point of view, most of Clive and Pete's songs have aged quite well. People, and the passions and frustrations that drive them, have not changed all that much. There are occasional practical details that have been overtaken by the march of history, in songs like 'Girl on the Train' ('Apart from the chance of the driver accepting a cheque / for crashing his loco so I could be brave in the wreck' and the quaint reference to the 'second class coach') and 'Have You Got a Biro I Can Borrow?' (when did you last see a biro made by Biro?). But, on the whole, there is little in the lyrics that needs to be explained for today's audiences.

The most obvious exceptions occur in 'Laughing Boy', a happy/sad Tears-of-a-Clown-type song Clive and Pete wrote in the late Sixties, when they were still students at Cambridge. In the second verse, there is an episode that is so thoroughly 1960s that it almost requires word-for-word translation for those who were not there at the time. It involves the hero being buttonholed by a girl collecting money for fireworks for Bonfire Night. This was a tradition that was still going strong all over the country at that time and continued in many places into the Seventies and early Eighties. No-one thought it remotely odd, at that time, that children of five or six or seven, including kids from middle class families, should be out on their own, accosting strangers in the street with the cry 'Penny for the guy, mister'. But there were strict conventions. A penny was what you asked for, and it was frowned on to take the pram with your home-made guy out onto the streets until a week or two before the Fifth of November.

So the girl who approaches the narrator in September and extorts a shilling, rather than a penny, from him is showing a fairly ambitious entrepreneurial spirit, leaving the man to gasp in admiration at her barefaced temerity.

A kid once asked me in late September for a shilling for the guy.

And I looked that little operator in her wheeling-dealing eye

And I tossed a bob with deep respect in her old man's trilby hat.

It seems to me that a man like me could die of things like that.

When the song was first written, the nuances of this encounter would have required no explanation. From today's perspective, though, it seems like a ritual from an alien world. As the number of homeless people seen on the streets of Britain rose in the Eighties, the tradition of collecting for Guy Fawkes Night died out and Halloween, in its North American guise, with masks, pumpkins and trick-or-treating, quickly became the focus of children's attention at this time of year. As ever, the Americans claimed long historical precedents for these traditions, though the phrase 'trick or treat' was actually unknown in the US until the 1930s. You can still see a few children collecting for the guy in some parts of the country, but the old conventions have been completely discarded. The last time I was approached, the urchin involved took out his earphones, gestured at a stuffed bin-liner with a hat on top and shouted 'Give us a pound, mister', in a tone of voice that sounded more like a threat than a request.

'Laughing Boy' is not the most original lyric Clive has ever written. The couplet that forms the chorus, 'I've got the only cure for life, and the cure for life is joy / I'm a crying man that everyone calls Laughing Boy', has always struck me as making too obvious a grab for the listener's sympathy. But he has always been particularly fond of this early song. On the all-too-rare occasions when the two of them have gone on tour together, in the UK, Australia and Hong

Kong, it has provided the opportunity for audiences to enjoy the unusual spectacle of Clive taking the microphone and singing in public, trading verses with Pete.

And there is a lot to admire within the lyrics. I like the details – the way the woman holds back her hair to light a cigarette and the girls who 'breathe on their fingernails and wiggle them in the air'. But it is the third verse that really hits the heights. The hero's need to rent a room brings him into contact with a generation of landladies whose lives have been lived out in the long shadow of the First World War.

> I've seen landladies who lost their lovers at the time of Rupert Brooke.
> And they pressed the flowers from Sunday rambles and then forgot
>   which book.
> And I paid the rent, thinking 'Anyway, buddy, at least you won't get wet.'
> And I tried the bed and lay there thinking 'They haven't got you yet'

This is great stuff, a whole ill-fated romance compressed into a couple of hugely evocative and effortlessly free-flowing lines. The effect is undoubtedly poetic, and there's no doubt that these eternally grieving landladies would have attracted a lot more attention if they had appeared in one of Clive's poems. In the song, their story is past and gone in a matter of seconds. But Clive has never forgotten them, and he did revisit the lost loves of earlier generations in a poem written more than forty years later.

'At the other end of my life,' he says, 'the landlady with the pressed flowers showed up again in my poem "Grief Has Its Time".'

This tells the tale of an incident at a book signing after Clive has been reading his poetry. An 'ancient lady', the last person in the queue, thanks him for making her smile 'the way *he* used to do' and asks him to sign his book for two people. 'Can you put his name with mine?' she says. 'Before the war, before he went away, we used to read together.'

It's not literally the landlady with the pressed flowers again, of course. With the passage of time, we have moved forward to the next generation, the ones who lost their hopes and dreams in World War II. But the ladies are poetic twins and both episodes – the pressed flowers in the song and the side-by-side names in the poem – are fine examples of Clive's ability to trigger powerful emotions through tiny cameos and quickly-sketched stories.

Laughing Boy

WORDS BY CLIVE JAMES, MUSIC BY PETE ATKIN

In all the rooms I've hung my hat, in all the towns I've been,
It stuns me I'm not dead already from the shambles that I've seen.
I've seen a girl hold back her hair to light a cigarette
And things like that a man like me can't easily forget.
I've got the only cure for life, and the cure for life is joy.
I'm a crying man that everyone calls Laughing Boy

A kid once asked me in late September for a shilling for the guy.
And I looked that little operator in her wheeling-dealing eye
And I tossed a bob with deep respect in her old man's trilby hat.

It seems to me that a man like me could die of things like that.

I've got the only cure for life, and the cure for life is joy.

I'm a crying man that everyone calls Laughing Boy

I've seen landladies who lost their lovers at the time of Rupert Brooke.

And they pressed the flowers from Sunday rambles and then forgot
which book.

And I paid the rent, thinking 'Anyway, buddy, at least you won't get wet.'

And I tried the bed and lay there thinking 'They haven't got you yet.'

I've got the only cure for life, and the cure for life is joy.

I'm a crying man that everyone calls Laughing Boy

I've read the labels on a hundred bottles for eyes and lips and hair.

And I've seen girls breathe on their fingernails and wiggle them in the air.

And I've often wondered who the hell remembers as far back as last night.

It seems to me that a man like me is the only one who might.

I've got the only cure for life, and the cure for life is joy.

I'm a crying man that everyone calls Laughing Boy

7

Cover Girl

In the Sixties and Seventies, great songwriters like Dylan, Joni Mitchell, Smokey Robinson and Randy Newman rarely sprang fully formed into the public consciousness.

Strange as it seems now, we discovered Bob Dylan through saccharine folk group Peter, Paul and Mary's cover of 'Blowing In the Wind', the follow-up to early hits like 'If I Had a Hammer' and 'Puff the Magic Dragon'. Smokey Robinson came to our attention via a few off-the-cuff remarks by John Lennon, followed by the Beatles' sensational cover of 'You've Really Got a Hold on Me' on the second album, *With the Beatles*. Joni Mitchell was a complete unknown until Judy Collins hit the US and UK charts with her bland version of 'Both Sides Now', while Randy Newman pumped out hits for artists such as Cilla Black (the exquisite 'I've Been Wrong Before'), Gene Pitney ('Just One Smile') and the Alan Price Set ('Simon Smith and the Amazing Dancing Bear') for several years before he finally made an album in his own right.

This indirect route to fame and fortune was so well established by the late Sixties that the first album of Pete Atkin/Clive James compositions was originally conceived as little more than a collection of demos from which, it was hoped, other artists would pick their favourites and produce successful cover versions. There was enthusiastic support for this approach from their publishers, Essex Music, and, in particular, from the company's German-born boss, David Platz. Platz had already proved his ability to spot the tunes and artists that mattered, with an impressive track record that included hits for the Rolling Stones, the Who, David Bowie and the Moody Blues. He had faith in the James/Atkin partnership, but he was as realistic as he was shrewd and he didn't hold back.

'If we couldn't get a hit single, he told us, our plan to make highbrow LPs would result in a long agony,' Clive wrote in his 2006 book, *North Face of Soho* (otherwise known as *Unreliable Memoirs, Take 4*).

Essex Music funded the recording of the album and licensed the tapes to the record company, Philips Fontana, who shared their belief that the fourteen tracks on the first album included several potential hits. Songs like 'Touch Has a Memory', 'Girl on the Train' and 'Tonight Your Love Is Over' – perhaps even 'Master of the Revels' and the title track, 'Beware of the Beautiful Stranger' – might be destined for greatness, if only they could be brought to the attention of the right performers. But this enthusiasm was tempered by an unsentimental reluctance to risk too much money on an unproven songwriting team. The album was made on a budget Clive describes as 'peanuts', banged out in a total of nine hours' recording time spread over three mornings at London's Regent Sound studios, off Tottenham Court Road. Small fry like Pete Atkin got the morning sessions because the established stars liked to drift in and start working some time in mid-afternoon.

'They couldn't get up,' says Clive. 'They thought the day started at lunchtime.'

As it turned out, the only two James/Atkin songs that were covered in the very early days were 'The Magic Wasn't There' and 'Tonight Your Love Is Over', which Julie Covington released as her first two singles on the Columbia label in 1970. Pete's own recording of 'Tonight Your Love Is Over' made it onto *Beware of the Beautiful Stranger*, but it was thirty years before his superb version of 'The Magic Wasn't There' became available. Even then, it was on Pete's privately-distributed double album, *The Lakeside Sessions*, which doomed it to finding only a small and select audience.

But back in 1970, Julie's single came very close to making the breakthrough. Her powerful voice, set against a big, confident string arrangement, played up the emotion in the song in ways Pete's original demo had hardly hinted at, while giving full weight to Clive's witty and original words. The record attracted a good deal of airplay and hovered tantalisingly close to the lower reaches of the charts for several weeks before slipping from view.

'I've often thought about how our songwriting career would have moved on if "The Magic Wasn't There" had broken through, which it nearly did,' says Pete. 'If it had been a medium-sized hit – maybe Number 14 in the charts, or something like that – I think we'd have been under a lot of record company pressure to write more songs like it. People were pretty unimaginative, and "Exactly the same, but somehow different" was what the industry demanded in those days. We'd have found that hard.

'We had a lot of different types of song that we wanted to write.

And I don't think Clive has ever got on well with the idea of delivering to an imposed brief, in any field he's worked in. In fact, I might have found it easier than him to buckle down and write that sort of commercial song to order.'

The problem didn't arise, of course, and Clive and Pete escaped with their integrity unsullied and their wallets unburdened. But the single had been heard by enough people to make an impact. On the strength of it, Julie Covington won the contract for her first album, *The Beautiful Changes*, made up almost entirely of Atkin/James songs and mainly recorded at the legendary Abbey Road studios. And Clive's most majestic line, 'How beautiful they are, the trains you miss' has become a much-quoted favourite (especially, and puzzlingly, among people in Holland, Google research reveals).

Though it's smuggled in, self-effacingly, under cover of someone else's genius ('Who was it then, the poet who once said...?'), I had always believed this was pure Clive James. It's taken me many decades to discover that it is actually a translation of a line ('Comme ils sont beaux, les trains manqués') from the 19th-century Uruguayan-born Symbolist poet Jules Laforgue, who was apparently a major influence on TS Eliot. So it's a classic example of Clive's magpie tendency, his delight in collecting and hoarding shiny objects and slipping them into his writing. Nicked or not, however, it is a great line. It sums up the theme of missed opportunities and the regrets they leave behind in a way that resonates long after the song has ended – a memorable and consciously poetic idea that contrasts with the conversational style of the rest of the lyric. But the whole song is a fine demonstration of the lessons Clive and Pete had already learned from the master songsmiths of Tin Pan Alley about pacing, control and the intimate fusion of words and music. It is crammed with unexpected ideas and memorable phrases. 'Some people vanish with a trace' Julie sings, 'And now what never happened drives me wild / Because the magic wasn't there.'

Listening to 'The Magic Wasn't There', which ultimately flopped, alongside Julie's 1977 hit, 'Don't Cry For Me Argentina', it is not immediately obvious why one took off and the other didn't, other than the fact that the Tim Rice/Andrew Lloyd-Webber song was promoted as the standard-bearer for the much-hyped *Evita* concept album. ('Don't Cry for Me Argentina' was originally, and potentially disastrously, titled 'It's Only Your Lover Returning'. It was only changed at playback stage, after the whole double album had been recorded, when Rice and Lloyd-Webber realised it was a dead duck of a line and called Julie Covington back into the studio to overdub the five words that turned the song into a hit.)

By the time *Evita* came around, Julie had developed a more dramatically intense delivery, stopping just short of melodrama, that would, in retrospect, have been equally appropriate for the Atkin/James number. But there's not all that much to choose between the songs, and the key difference may ultimately have been one of timing. If the British public had been in the right mood for 'The Magic Wasn't There' in 1970, Pete and Clive might have found their careers heading in a very different direction.

The Magic Wasn't There

WORDS BY CLIVE JAMES, MUSIC BY PETE ATKIN

With just a word, a single sign of care,
With just a touch, I could have been beguiled.
But circumstances never smiled
Because the magic wasn't there

Who was it then, the poet who once said
'How beautiful they are, the trains you miss'?
So time can't put an end to this.
I have the memory instead

These nothing scenes are still experience.
You even weep for what did not take place.
Events that don't occur are still events.
Some people vanish with a trace

With just a word, a single sign of care,
With just a touch, I could have been beguiled.
But circumstances never smiled
Because the magic wasn't there

With just a word, a single sign of care,
With just a touch, I could have been beguiled.
But circumstances never smiled
And now what never happened drives me wild,

Because the magic wasn't there.

The magic wasn't there.

The magic wasn't there

8

Touching Memories

Pete's recording career began while he and Clive were still at university, in the late 1960s, with two privately-pressed vinyl LPs. The first was *While the Music Lasts*, which featured twelve songs of Pete's, including five co-written with Clive, and one historical oddity, 'The Paper Wing Song', the only song ever for which Clive James wrote both the words and the music. Pete shared the singing with Julie Covington and the album was recorded in 1967 in the Footlights Clubroom in Cambridge, with strategically-draped blankets to damp down the room's natural echo, and released in a (very) limited edition of 160 copies.

The second album from the Cambridge days was *The Party's Moving On*, which they made in 1969. This had 24 tracks and it was recorded in a proper studio in London, though this time the production run was even smaller. Just 99 copies were pressed. The law had recently been changed and any run of 100 copies or more now attracted purchase tax (the forerunner of VAT), so staying below that threshold saved money, which could then be invested in lavish production values.

'We paid for a glossy cardboard front cover, stuck onto the front of the record sleeve by hand,' says Pete. 'It made our record look like a proper commercial LP, unless you looked closely.'

The music, though, was sensational. Again, Pete and Julie Covington shared the singing, more or less 50/50. The arrangements were simple – just Pete on piano or guitar and Steve Cook on bass – but the roster of top-quality songs was astounding for a privately made album, providing abundant and early evidence of the potential of this blossoming songwriting partnership. The album introduced many songs that were to become Atkin/James classics, including 'Girl on the Train' (later voted Best Song in an online poll of Atkin fans), 'Practical Man', 'You Can't Expect to Be Remembered' and 'Have You Got a Biro I Can Borrow?', alongside Julie's original version of 'The Magic Wasn't There'.

I remember hearing 'Have You Got a Biro I Can Borrow?' for the first time in the packed crypt of our folk club. I fell in love with the song straight away, dazzled and delighted by its playful inventiveness. I loved the way the imagination's camera zoomed back in stages from the intimate close-up ('I'd like to write your name / On the palm of my hand') to wider and wider shots ('On the walls of the hall / The roof of the house, right across the land') and on out to the ultimate romantic image of the girl's name written across the face of the sun. I liked the middle eight, with its jaunty exploration of all the creative ways the narrator might express his passion (and its classy reference to the aged and arthritic Renoir, racked with pain, painting his last canvases with a brush bound to his twisted and deformed fingers).

Oh give me a pen and some paper.

Give me a chisel or a camera,

A piano and a box of rubber bands.

I need room for choreography

And a darkroom for photography.

Tie the brush into my hands

Above all, I was charmed by the elegance and finely-worked crafts-manship of the last verse. Clive's dancing constellation of internal rhymes ('From the belt of Orion to the share of the Plough / The snout of the Bear to the belly of the Lion') seemed like poetic writing of the highest order, yet it was worked into a simple, hummable song that made no great claims for itself. And the ending – 'There'll never be a minute, / Not a moment of the night, that hasn't got you in it' – struck me as one of the most persuasively romantic ideas a young lover could ever come up with.

In the midst of all these gems, *The Party's Moving On* also included the first of Pete's three studio recordings of the strikingly original 'Touch Has a Memory'.

Clive's lyric for this steals a line from John Keats as its starting point, taken from a strange and florid poem that throws off unusual ideas in all directions but never quite gets round to making the most of any of them. Keats actually uses the phrase 'Touch has a memory', but he doesn't get as far as Clive's insight that tactile memories have a special quality of persistence. You can't fight the impression of touch when it happens ('Touching has no defences'). And you can't erase the memory when it's over. Sights and sounds will fade with time, but, as the repeated line in the first and third verse says: 'Textures come back to you real as can be'.

A year after *The Party's Moving On*, when Pete made his first commercial album, *Beware of the Beautiful Stranger*, 'Touch Has a Memory' was singled out for special treatment. It's a slow song anyway, but this time it was chilled right down to hibernation tempo, making it 60 per cent longer, and given a classical feel, with violins, cellos and double bass in a lush string arrangement and no guitar or percussion in sight. Many people enjoyed the change of pace and Pete was initially delighted with the recording. Over time, however, he came to regret taking this approach. And when RCA Records repackaged and reissued *Beware of the Beautiful Stranger*, just three years later, Pete added the upbeat 'Be Careful When They Offer You the Moon' instead and dropped 'Touch Has a Memory' altogether.

'In the end, the richness of the string arrangement didn't compensate for the loss of the rhythmic impetus the demo version had,' he says. 'That's why we left it off the original reissue – not because we didn't still like the song, but because we did. If you follow me.'

Fans have always liked it, too, and the more patient and longlived enthusiasts had their reward in 2007 when a remade 'Touch Has a Memory' took pride of place as the first track on *Midnight Voices*, the excellent 'greatest hits' album. This version is not actually played much faster than the one with the strings, but it is light, airy and relaxed, with lots of space around the lines (including a full instrumental verse before the vocals come in) and room for a breathy, lyrical tenor sax solo by Alan Barnes and gently supportive piano by Pete's old friend Simon Wallace. Allowing more space for the music to come through like this makes the song longer again. At 3 minutes 22 seconds, it's twice the length of the original 1969 demo version.

For those of us who have liked this song for forty years or more, there is something contained and perfect about 'Touch Has a Memory'. The words are simple and direct, tightly rhymed, with just three verses and no middle eight. It doesn't just talk about touching, though. The key couplet ('Eyelids are modest, yet blink at a kiss / Touching takes note of this') is a vivid reminder of an exquisite moment of intimacy. And there is something delicately wonderful about the way the syntax unfolds in the last stanza. After two verses in which each new idea is given exactly two lines, the grammatical structure and the rhythm change slightly. The first four lines of this last verse are all one longer sentence ('When, in a later day, little of the vision lingers, memory slips away every way but through the fingers') and the movement of that eight-syllable line ('Every way but through the fingers') is quite different from that of the seven-syllable lines that occur at this point in the two earlier verses.

Whether Clive consciously created that effect or not isn't important. It may just have been the spontaneous result of his instinct and feeling for words. But it works splendidly, setting up the last two lines before the song ends where it began, 'And touch has a memory'. Those lines just before the end are interesting in themselves. In the previous verses, there are conventional end-of-line rhymes ('be' and 'memory', 'kiss' and 'this'). But here it is an internal rhyme ('real') that rhymes with 'feel', internally, and eventually with 'heal', the last syllable of the next line. That was deliberate, and it shows a craftsmanlike finesse that marks its author out as one of the best lyric writers of our time.

Touch Has a Memory

WORDS BY CLIVE JAMES, MUSIC BY PETE ATKIN

Touch has a memory,

Better than the other senses.

Hearing and sight fight free.

Touching has no defences.

Textures come back to you real as can be.

Touch has a memory

Fine eyes are wide at night,

Eyelashes show that nicely.

Seeing forgets the sight,

Touch recollects precisely.

Eyelids are modest, yet blink at a kiss.

Touching takes note of this

When, in a later day,

Little of the vision lingers,

Memory slips away

Every way but through the fingers.

Textures come back to you real as can be,

Making you feel time doesn't heal.

And touch has a memory

9

The Singer or the Song?

As a singer, Pete Atkin does not believe in melodrama. His voice is accurate, flexible and pleasant, but he sounds defiantly British, without a trace of the standard American or mid-Atlantic accent adopted by virtually all his contemporaries. He is an interpreter, rather than a star.

'From the start, we thought of ourselves as writers,' he says. 'I was a performer, too, of course, in those early Cambridge Footlights shows, but that wasn't what I planned to do with my life. I didn't even have a plan to make records. As far as I was concerned, performing was just what I had to do to present our songs and get other people to think about recording them.'

As it happened, that traditional relationship between songsmiths and performers was one of the aspects of the music business that was changing abruptly in the late Sixties.

'When we started thinking about how to get our songs out to the world, it didn't occur to us to talk to record companies,' says Pete. 'I was taking our stuff round to publishers. I thought they were the key. If we had the publishers on our side, surely they'd push our songs and find artists who wanted to record them.'

But the Beatles had changed all that. Everyone in the business could see that the big money lay in finding artists who would write and perform their own songs.

If you look at what was in the Hit Parade during the mid-to-late Sixties, it was an extraordinarily rich time. And it wasn't just the very best stuff, the classics from Lennon and McCartney and Bob Dylan. All kinds of remarkable, memorable songs were being churned out from all directions.

In one week in December 1965, for example, the Top 30 chart featured 'Day Tripper' and 'My Generation', the Stones' 'Get Off My Cloud' and Dylan's 'Positively 4th Street', 'Keep On Running' by the Spencer Davis Group and singles by the Kinks, the Animals, Otis Redding and Elvis Presley.

Move on six months and it's much the same. The Top Ten alone included 'Strangers in the Night', 'Paperback Writer', 'When a Man Loves a Woman' and 'Wild Thing', plus contributions from the Stones, the Mamas & the Papas, the Animals and the Yardbirds. There wasn't room for much rubbish, though Ken Dodd's gruesome 'Promises' was a sobering reminder that old people with tin ears bought records, too.

As a student, Pete was steadily working his way through the college record library, listening to everything he could find from people like the Gershwins, Cole Porter, Rodgers and Hart, Jerome Kern and Duke Ellington.

'I was hearing all these amazing singles as they came out, week by week, and discovering the great tradition of Tin Pan Alley song-writing at the same time. So I was getting the Beatles in one ear and the eight classic Ella Fitzgerald songbook albums in the other.

'When Clive and I started writing songs, one of the things that excited us was the idea of bringing those two traditions together. We wanted to find a way to combine the ambition and craftsmanship of the old songs with the sheer power of 1960s pop.

'We loved what the great songwriters did with the words – the ingenuity, the simplicity and the sheer class of Cole Porter, Lorenz Hart, Johnny Mercer and the rest of them. And we loved what was happening in post-Beatles rock – the energy and the freedom that Lennon and McCartney had unleashed.

'We didn't see any reason why these things shouldn't be brought together. And we hoped we might be the people to do it.'

'I don't know that we managed it very often, but that was the motivation. We were living in a time that was tremendously exciting, musically. What we didn't know, then, was that it was a one-off, that things would never be quite like this again. There'd never be another time when the pop music scene was so intensely creative and the mainstream audience was so open to new ideas.'

There are certain cultural moments when a new or much-changed art form suddenly becomes the natural mode of expression for people with something to say. It happened in late Elizabethan times, when the first theatres were built in London, starting with The Theatre in 1576 and followed, before the end of the century, by the Curtain (which, of course, had no curtains), the Rose, the Swan and the Globe. A golden generation – Shakespeare, Marlowe, Kyd, Jonson and the rest of them – more or less invented English drama overnight, found an audience that crossed all barriers of class and education and achieved fame and rock star status. But the groundlings who flocked to the Globe didn't know they were living in a golden age. Nobody told them. They probably thought this was how it would always be, with each of the main theatre companies pumping out thirty or forty new plays a year, scoring hit after hit and performing to packed houses night after night. But the moment was fleeting. It only lasted twenty years or so before the revolution ran out of steam and lost its momentum.

People can argue about where to draw the line, but the pop revolution that started when the Beatles broke through in 1963 had certainly run its course by the early Seventies. As the music industry grew, it became less spontaneous and more cynical – leading, incidentally, to one of the funniest James/Atkin creations, 'Practical Man', a cartoon strip of a song in which a budding young artist is wined, dined and invited to sell his soul by a thoroughly pragmatic and shamelessly philistine showbiz executive.

'I'll see you right,' said the Practical Man,
'A boy like you should be living high.
All you do is get up and be funny
And I'll turn the laughs into folding money.
Can you name me anything that can't buy?'

'So you deal in dreams,' said the Practical Man.
'So does that mean you should be so coy?
I fixed one chap a show on telly
Who limped like Byron and talked like Shelley
Through a ten-part epic on the Fall of Troy'

As the accountants and the Practical Men took over, Clive and Pete recognised that winning a record deal was going to be essential in the new environment. The industry was suddenly obsessed with singer/songwriters, so Pete's ability to take the songs out on the road, build an audience and promote albums through live tours was an essential part of the package.

In the song, the Practical Man is clearly educated, as well as cynical. He knows about Byron's club foot and Shelley's voice (some sharp-tongued 19th-century Clive James called it a 'cracked soprano') but he's not about to let culture get in the way of commerce. The impoverished singer, Wild Creative Fool that he is, nobly resists the temptations dangled before him, in a way Clive describes now as 'the merest posturing', ending the conversation with the line 'There are just some songs that are not for sale'.

'We would dearly have liked to sell some songs, if only to keep eating,' the Wild Colonial Boy says, in a note about 'Practical Man' in his new *Collected Poems*. 'But the music business in those days was all against it, because we had started writing songs to be sung by other people at the exact moment in history when the singers had started writing their own songs so that they could be paid twice.'

The Practical Man Pete and Clive needed to meet – the one who was sensitive enough to recognise their potential but knowing enough about the practicalities of the music business to market it effectively – has always eluded them. Indeed, their relationship with their first agent ended in tears, with recriminations and injunctions ('We signed up with the first agent who walked in the door, and that's the last person you should ever sign anything with,' says Clive).

But they did eventually get the record deals, first with Philips Fontana and then with RCA, that led to six classic albums in five years. The deals were unprofitable and the record company support was all talk, but these LPs did put 73 of their songs out into the world to be heard and treasured by the fans and studiously neglected by the public at large. The original Philips version of the second record, *Driving Through Mythical America*, often changes hands on the internet at eye-watering prices – sometimes up to £200 – causing Pete to wince at the irony of it all. His own income from sales of the same album added up to just £50.

Clive's noticed the online demand, too.

'We have always been big on eBay,' he says. 'We've never had a problem with the secondhand market. It's the firsthand market we've struggled with.'

When the RCA contract ran out, after *Live Libel*, there was no long queue of record companies rushing to sign up an awkwardly uncategorisable songwriting team with creative ambitions that were so out of step with the times.

Punk was just beginning to flex its attitudes, and the wordy, witty eccentricities of Elvis Costello (probably the nearest thing to Clive and Pete ever to hit the pop charts) had not yet made their mark. The music business didn't know what to do with them and no deal was done.

'I'd fulfilled my contract and RCA offered me a renewal, but I, in my lofty way, declined the offer and decided we should go elsewhere,' says Pete. 'The whole industry was in a state of panic, mesmerised by the arrival of this new movement, punk, in a way that has never happened since, and all the record companies wanted was to get themselves a roster of punk bands.

'With the benefit of hindsight, I can see it was always the idea that there was another album in the offing that spurred us on to write new songs. Without that, we carried on writing, but our output tapered off. Everything changed. We never decided to stop writing, but it just happened.'

As Clive's journalistic and television careers gathered pace, Pete retreated from the endless round of underpaid folk club and college gigs. He took to working as a carpenter (and writing a DIY tips column for the UK's first 'green' magazine, *Vole*), before almost accidentally joining BBC Light Entertainment and becoming a highly successful radio producer, producing *Just a Minute*, *My Word!* and *Week Ending* and, later, as a freelance, Radio 4's huge 216-part history of Britain, *This Sceptred Isle*.

As always, life threw up quite enough obstacles and opportunities to destroy the original blueprint Pete and Clive had laid down for their careers. The dream of becoming known, and solvent, on the strength of their songwriting faded slowly, though it was never quite extinguished. But how different it might have been if they had met the right Practical Man at the right time.

Practical Man

WORDS BY CLIVE JAMES, MUSIC BY PETE ATKIN

Last night I drank with a Practical Man
Who seemed to think he knew me well.
He had no debts and he had no troubles.
All night long he kept setting up doubles
And he asked me 'What have you got to sell?'

'I'll see you right,' said the Practical Man.
'A boy like you should be living high.
All you do is get up and be funny
And I'll turn the laughs into folding money.
Can you name me anything that can't buy?'

'So you deal in dreams,' said the Practical Man.
'So does that mean you should be so coy?
I fixed one chap a show on telly
Who limped like Byron and talked like Shelley
Through a ten-part epic on the Fall of Troy.'

'I'll tell you what,' said the Practical Man,
As he tapped the ash from a purple fag,
'Let's head uptown for a meal somewhere.
You can sing me something while we're driving there.
There's a grand piano in the back of my Jag.'

THE SINGER OR THE SONG?

So I sang my song to the Practical Man.
It sounded bad, but she couldn't hear.
And the silent lights of town went streaming,
As if the car was a turtle dreaming.
The night was sad and she was nowhere near

'It's a great idea,' said the Practical Man,
As they brought in waiters on flaming swords.
'You love this chick and it's really magic,
But she won't play ball. That's kind of tragic.
Now, how do we get this concept on the boards?'

'I see it like this,' said the Practical Man,
As he chose a trout from the restaurant pool.
'We change it round so she's going frantic
To win the love of the last romantic.
And you're the one, her wild creative fool.'

So I thought it all over as the Practical Man
Watched them slaughter the fatted calf.
I saw again her regretful smile,
Sweet to look at, though it meant denial.
It was bound to hurt, but I had to laugh

And that's when I told the Practical Man,
As he drank champagne from the Holy Grail,
'There are some ideas you can't play round with,

Can't let go of and you can't give ground with.
'Cause when you die, they're what you're found with.
There are just some songs that are not for sale'

10

Cottonmouth

In 1973, a young rock critic, Charles Shaar Murray, bashed out a magnificently passionate article for *Cream* magazine about the Eurovision Song Contest, deploring the oompah tendency and massed pop clichés that characterised every country's Eurovision entries and asking why we couldn't have proper songs, rather than the identikit confections that turned up year after year. This was before Abba's 'Waterloo', at a time when Eurovision could hardly claim to have launched a single significant musical career, and his anger at the wasted opportunity crackled off the page.

'Think of the songwriters we've got in this country,' Murray wrote. 'David Bowie, Elton John and Bernie Taupin, Cat Stevens, Lennon, O'Sullivan, the Bee Gees, McCartney, James and Atkin, Pete Townshend, Roy Wood, Jack Bruce and Pete Brown, Jagger and Richards – there ain't exactly a shortage of folks who can turn out a nice tune when they want to.'

One or two of these names have faded over time. Roy Wood, who created a long string of catchy, quirky pop hits for the Move, ELO and Wizzard (including 'Fire Brigade', 'Brontosaurus' and 'See My Baby Jive'), is mainly remembered now for 'I Wish It Could Be Christmas

Everyday'. Gilbert O'Sullivan is largely forgotten (except by Morrissey, who often performs his song 'Nothing Rhymed') and the writing partnership of Jack Bruce and Pete Brown doesn't ring a lot of bells, until it is pointed out that they co-wrote many of Cream's biggest tracks, including (with Clapton) 'Sunshine of Your Love'. In their day, though, they all achieved fame and fortune on a grand scale. Every single one of them. Except, of course, James and Atkin, who managed to dodge the perils of songwriting success with surefooted ease.

Pete remembers seeing the Charles Shaar Murray article when it first came out. Surely an endorsement like that in the trendiest music magazine of its day would help them break through. He was hopping up and down with excitement.

'Just to be included in that company was a great honour,' he says. 'These were the people who were pushing the boundaries in all sorts of different directions, while still getting through to a big audience. And there we were – not even as an afterthought, but tucked in there right in the middle of the list.'

They were there on merit, too, purely on the basis of the quality of their songs. Their record companies, first Philips Fontana, then RCA, hardly lifted a finger to back them, and people searching for the albums often found the record shops were out of stock. The reviews were almost always good, and sometimes ecstatic, but the business didn't know how to promote them and couldn't be bothered to find out. Even when Clive's media career began to take off, that wasn't the advantage it might have been. As his star rose, attitudes towards his songwriting became surprisingly hostile and patronising.

'That Charles Shaar Murray article was before Clive was known for anything else,' Pete says. 'But as soon as he became famous on television, people started discounting his work. He became a target for that curious British snobbery that objects to anyone trying to do more than one thing. The Americans aren't like that. They applaud people for working across several different fields. A lot of the press and critics got quite sniffy about Clive.

'The songs were just ignored by the critics. And they still are. Not one of the reviews I've seen of Clive's new *Collected Poems* has mentioned the thirty song lyrics that are included in the book. They're just blanked.'

It's probably true that Clive's current standing as a poet of real worth and significance couldn't have been achieved if he hadn't taken the decision, at the turn of the millennium, to walk away from his television career. He was writing serious poetry, as well as intelligent and well-argued essays and criticism, for years before he ducked out of the spotlight, but the populist television persona made it all too easy for people to dismiss him as a lightweight jack-of-all-trades, without ever taking the trouble to read his work properly. Even fellow journalists who knew him and were aware of his formidable intellect often gave way to the temptation to write about the man and his image, rather than what he produced.

Clive has made enemies, occasionally, and sometimes even rejoiced in his ability to rub people up the wrong way. He has been outspoken, often, and wrong, from time to time. He's talked too much, probably, and taken too much delight in his own eloquence. But none of this would surprise anyone who had heard Pete sing one of the early songs, from the mid-Seventies, called 'Cottonmouth'.

This song was written in 1974 and was lined up to be one of the tracks on Pete Atkin's seventh commercial album, the one that never happened. He played it on live gigs, but there was no recorded version at all until 2015's CD, *The Colours of the Night*. And though it is not Clive's finest song, it is, he says, 'among the more deeply autobiographical of my lyrics'.

Despite its innocuous-sounding name, the cottonmouth is a dangerous snake, a type of pit viper with a bad temper and a potentially fatal bite, that's found in the Southeastern United States. So it's hardly a complimentary nickname. And the tone of the song is nothing if not ambiguous. It's almost jaunty, in a deadpan sort of way, but that is offset and undermined by the sinuous, sinister, insinuating slipperiness of Chris Spedding's serpentine slide guitar.

In the song, the thinly-disguised hero has a number of specific attributes. He is a fast-thinking, fast-talking phrasemaker, rash, flirtatious, clever, sentimental and, the lyrics repeat, 'absolutely insane'. He claims to be shy, but says 'the first thing that occurred' and obviously takes pride in running rings round his listeners. There are not many autobiographical songs that take such a critical and nuanced view of the person they are describing. But Clive is even-handed. He knows his ability to turn a fine phrase is both a blessing and a burden, and he understands that other people ('simple, downright and sincere') are not necessarily charmed by the show of wit and eloquence.

'I really was, or so I supposed, the talker who had to change countries because he couldn't stop talking,' he wrote, in his sleeve notes to *The Colours of the Night*.

Clive's insistence that 'Cottonmouth' is autobiographical ('written a long time ago, looking ahead') contrasts with Pete's account of the song. When he's played it on stage, he has sometimes introduced it as a number from a projected, and unwritten, Atkin/James musical, 'the character song for the musical's bad guy'.

'It's about a very nasty person indeed,' he says. 'But to be perverse I'd occasionally write a bright, cheerful, tune for one of Clive's grimmer lyrics. This was an example of that.'

In fact, of course, as Pete and Clive have both said many times, the writer is the last person you should ask about what a song really means. Whatever the impulse that led to its composition, it becomes something out there, on its own, separate from its creator. The imaginary musical never existed. It was just Pete's way of framing the song, setting up a mood and an attitude for the audience. And Clive's assertion that the song was about him should be taken with an equally generous pinch of salt. You can see where the process that led to the 'Cottonmouth' lyric began, but this is songwriting, not news reporting. The gypsy in 'Beware of the Beautiful Stranger' didn't really have a fully-functioning time-travelling multi-media crystal ball. When the hero of this song packs up and does a fade, he doesn't literally turn edgeways on and vanish like a razor blade. There's artistic licence at play here – not to mention wonderfully unexpected visual imagery. Whether the character in the song is wholly or partly based on Clive's view of himself is not the point. As the old Motown slogan used to say: 'It's what's in the grooves that counts.'

Cottonmouth

WORDS BY CLIVE JAMES, MUSIC BY PETE ATKIN

Cottonmouth had such a way of saying things.

Phrases used to fly like they were wearing wings.

Never had to weigh a word,

Said the first thing that occurred.

And round your head the stuff he said went running rings

Cottonmouth, what a brain.

Absolutely insane

Cottonmouth would tell the girls he sighed for them.

He talked of all the lonely nights he cried for them.

Afterwards they told their men,

'I just saw Cottonmouth again.

That guy's a scream.' They never guessed he died for them

Cottonmouth, what a brain.

Absolutely insane

Cottonmouth, what a guy.

He used to say he was shy,

So shy he could die

COTTONMOUTH

Cottonmouth packed up one day and did a fade.

Turned edgeways on and vanished like a razor blade.

Considering how people here

Are simple, downright and sincere,

It could have been the smartest move he ever made

Cottonmouth, what a brain.

Absolutely insane

11

Our Night with Sarah

In the early Seventies, the Tory government finally gave the green light for commercial broadcasting as an alternative to the BBC. The offshore pirate radio ships, Radio Caroline and 'wonderful Radio London, whoopee', had already changed the face of music radio and launched the careers of DJs like Tony Blackburn, Emperor Rosko, Kenny Everett and John Peel.

I was busy laying the foundations for my own journalistic career and I hadn't seen Clive or Pete for some time when I got a call from London's entertainment station, Capital Radio. Would I like to be one of the guests on Sarah Ward's all-night show next Saturday, talking about folk and rock music and anything else that came up, for the entertainment of a tiny night-time audience of insomniacs, minicab drivers and security guards? I could bring along my Geordie friend Frank McConnell, a co-founder of the Hanging Lamp folk club and a deft and witty fingerpicking guitarist, who would break the monotony with a few live songs in the course of the night. The other main guest would be Clive James, so there were unlikely to be too many unfilled gaps in the conversation, wherever it led.

I was delighted. Clive had never gone along to many of Pete's gigs and his own rise to fame, as the presenter of Granada TV's *Cinema* programme, a job he'd taken over from Michael Parkinson, had meant that he was now more likely to pop up in the corner of your living room than in a folk club. It would be good to meet up with him again, and I was so stagestruck that the thought of several hours with a microphone, a sweaty studio and a minute and bleary-eyed audience was irresistible.

It was a long haul. The show started at one o'clock in the morning and went right through to six. But there was an added complication on this particular night. It was late autumn and the clocks were due to go back. So we talked and listened to some music and talked some more, and when it got to 2am, we watched as the clocks were wound back and we had to do the same hour all over again.

I can't remember many details of the conversation now, but I know we touched on Beethoven, the blues and Bryan Ferry, and I'm sure Clive managed to squeeze Dante in there somehow. So we chatted and Frank sang and the occasional drowsy or hyperanimated call came in from the usual cast of late-night oddballs in Leytonstone and Bexley.

As I started to flag and Sarah Ward downed handfuls of pills that made her pupils dilate alarmingly, Clive led us on through the long night. Relaxed and effortlessly amusing, he seemed to get stronger as the hours went by. As both his writing and his songs have demonstrated over the years, Clive's extraordinarily wide range of interests and ideas meant he was never at a loss for a new angle. I remember thinking then, and it's still true today, that I'd never met anyone in my life who could dance so lightly across such a vast spectrum of subjects.

But as our defences sagged, the conversation was smoothly and elegantly hijacked, shifting gradually but inexorably away from music and towards the movies. I couldn't contribute much there, as I've always had the retentive capacity of a goldfish when it comes to remembering the films I've seen. Even now, the last movie I can clearly recall is *Out of Africa*. But Clive's *Cinema* duties had begun to include interviews with some of the big beasts of the silver screen and he regaled us for the last hours of the interminable night with behind-the-scenes tales of his recent encounters. He'd met Richard Burton ('head the size of a tea chest'), Burt Lancaster ('so much presence that everyone else felt absent') and Peter Sellers (drinking nothing over lunch but 'some special water that had to be brought in by courier from high in the Himalayas, where it had been strained through the loincloth of a swami') and this was sensational stuff. The programme came to life and the switchboard lit up with calls from all over the London area. By the time six o'clock came, it hardly mattered that no-one else in the studio had said anything much for the previous ninety minutes. As Sarah Ward – looking like death then, but still broadcasting regularly on Jazz FM forty years later – closed the show and we shuffled out into the night, Clive asked our hostess how she felt it had gone.

'It wasn't quite what I was expecting,' she said, 'But it was great. Thanks, Clive. That was a very different sort of all-nighter.'

By this point in his career, of course, Clive was a walking encyclopaedia of movie history. And it was about this time that he and Pete drew on this huge reservoir of film folklore to write one of their most immediately engaging songs.

'Screen-Freak' is an impressionistic collage of nearly forty historic movie references, set over a gentle waltz tune that wafts down like a falling leaf and leads into a pretty, lilting chorus. Audiences have always loved it, and you can hear the chuckles of delight and recognition as the fleeting images of Hollywood history flicker by. Strictly speaking, the lyrics hardly make sense, but that's not the point. Like 'I Am the Walrus' or 'American Pie', 'Screen-Freak' merges words and music to operate at a level that defies dissection.

When Don McLean was asked to explain the lyrics of 'American Pie', he said 'They're beyond analysis. They're poetry.' It's not always wise to take too much notice of McLean's comments – once, when he was asked what 'American Pie' meant, he replied, 'It means I don't ever have to work again' – but he had a point. Songs can work at a different level from prose. In its own way, 'Screen-Freak' does for the movies what 'American Pie' did for pop and rock music.

'Screen-Freak' is obviously a catalogue song, part of a great tradition that stretches back to early folk and broadside ballads and includes American classics like 'You're the Top'. But Clive's trademark inventiveness and ear for a telling phrase make the kaleidoscopic stream of namechecks and images more than just a list. 'My mind's eye's skies are glittering and white,' the narrator complains, in a fit of inspired assonance, and the Maltese Falcon falls 'moulting to the street'. There's a strange, dreamlike eroticism in the repeated chorus ('Dance, Ginger, dance / The kaftan of the Caliph turns to powder at your glance') and the image of Ginger Rogers, turning slowly to the accompaniment of a tinkling musical box tune, evokes a delicate balance of sensual poise and formal precision.

'Screen-Freak' also includes one neatly-turned couplet its author has always been particularly proud of. 'I've seen the plywood cities meet their doom because of dames / Atlantis down in bubbles and Atlanta up in flames' makes a wonderfully unexpected link between Plato's drowned civilisation and the Southern city burned to the ground by Sherman's troops in the American Civil War. The names are so similar that the connection seems obvious when it's pointed out, but it's the kind of association you can live half a lifetime without noticing, until someone like Clive comes along and nudges it into your consciousness.

Pete's arrangement uses an odd combination of elements – tuba, strings, wah-wah guitar (played by Chris Spedding) and Elton John's virtuoso percussionist, Ray Cooper, on glockenspiel. It creates shimmering, sensuous textures of light and shade, and it frames and spotlights Clive's imagery with effortless grace. The result is a charming, instantly likeable song that must surely have had the potential to become a hit. In 1973, when RCA decided to put out its first Atkin/James single, 'Screen-Freak' was paired with 'Carnations on the Roof', but the double A-side failed to make an impact, despite attracting the attention of several influential DJs.

There can be a hundred reasons why a good song misses its audience, but in this case it may simply have been the song's title. By calling it 'Screen-Freak', Clive and Pete broke one of the Nine Rules of Popular Song Writing that had been spelt out by Irving Berlin way back in 1925. Nobody knows everything in the music business, but the Old Master knew a lot more than most.

'Your title should be simple and easily remembered and should be planted in the body of the song,' he said. 'It should be emphasised and accented again and again. The public buys songs, not because it likes the song, but because it knows and likes the title idea.'

The title 'Screen-Freak' is a label. The words are not sung at any point. If only the title had been 'Dance, Ginger, Dance', there is surely a chance that this lovely little song would have benefited from the way the music and the words reinforced each other to catch the public ear and find the popularity it has always deserved.

Screen-Freak

WORDS BY CLIVE JAMES, MUSIC BY PETE ATKIN

You've got to help me, Doc, I see things in the night.
The tatters of my brain are bleached with flashing light.
Just the way Orion's sword is pumping stars in flight.
My mind's eye's skies are glittering and white

The Lady in the Dark has shot the Lady from Shanghai.
The Thin Man and the Quiet Man are Comin' Thro' the Rye.
At Red Line Seven Thousand there's No Highway In The Sky.
The villains are the deepest but they plumb refuse to die

Dance, Ginger, dance.
The kaftan of the Caliph turns to powder at your glance

The Ambersons have spiked the punch and livened up the ball,
Cagney's getting big and Sidney Greenstreet's getting small.
The Creature from the Black Lagoon left puddles in the hall
And Wee Willie Winkie is the most evil of them all

Strangers on a Wagon Train have crashed the China Gate.
The Portrait of Jennie has decided not to wait.
The Flying Leathernecks arrived a half a reel too late.
The Broadcast wasn't big enough and Ziegfeld wasn't great

    Dance, Ginger, dance.
    The kaftan of the Caliph turns to powder at your glance.
    This one for Funny Face and Fancy Pants

The love of Martha Ivers caused the death of Jesse James.
Kitty Foyle guessed it, though she didn't link their names.
I've seen the plywood cities meet their doom because of dames,
Atlantis down in bubbles and Atlanta up in flames

And I've seen the Maltese Falcon falling moulting to the street.
He was caught by Queen Christina who was Following the Fleet.
And Scarface found the Sleep was even Bigger than the Heat
When he hit the Yellow Brick Road to where the Grapes of Wrath are sweet

    Dance, Ginger, dance.
    The kaftan of the Caliph turns to powder at your glance.
    This one for Funny Face and Fancy Pants.
    A buck and wing might fix the Broken Lance
    And break my trance

12

Carnations on the Roof

When Clive James first arrived in London from Sydney, in the early Sixties, he saw rather more of life than he expected to. Bouncing around a string of jobs, as a library clerk, a market research interviewer and a circus roustabout, he glimpsed the world of work from a number of interesting angles. He was also employed for a time as a sheet metal worker at a factory in Holloway, a grimy, harsh, unrewarding job that made a deep impression on him, especially when he realised that this was the kind of career that so many people have to put up with for most of a lifetime.

Back home in Australia, he had grown up among the drills, gauges and spirit levels left behind in his father's toolbox when the recently-released POW was killed in a plane crash on his way home from imprisonment in Japan. Clive never had the chance to get to know his father, but he saw the devastating effect on his mother and he grew up in the shadow of this man, who had worked as a mechanic through the hard years of the Depression and volunteered to fight the Japanese without waiting for his call-up. The young boy played with the metal-working tools and dreamed of becoming a machinist, but it was not until he found himself working for peanuts in the

North London factory that he actually experienced the grit and reality of this kind of work. It made a lasting impression which surfaced, a few years later, in one of the most powerful songs on the third Pete Atkin album, *A King at Nightfall*.

The most striking feature of 'Carnations on the Roof' is its precisely observed detail. It presents a vivid, factually accurate description of life in the machine shop, full of motion, noise and colour, rushed lunchtime conversations about kids, bills and football, and a careful, dedicated concentration on the job in hand. We are shown the multi-purpose punch, the micrometer and other measuring tools. We feel the unstoppable rhythm of the machines – the chuck and punch 'pulsing like a drum'. We see the eerily green Swarfega cleaning jelly, the metal slugs like coins and the cutting-oil like scum. We watch the workers, hardly able to hear themselves think, passing on instructions in gestures, making 'signals like the dumb'. It's an oppressive, demanding environment, and the everyday heroism that's on show here might make you think, for a few seconds, that Clive was romanticising the life of the working man.

But this isn't a song about a working man's life. It's about his death – or, to be more precise, his funeral.

The carnations on the roof are flowers on a hearse and the man's epitaph ('generally respected') is not much reward for forty years' work on the shop floor. Conned into believing in the Dignity of Labour as a substitute for proper pay, he has sold his life short and ended up 'used and discarded' in a fat Austin Princess on its way to the crematorium.

This is one of the few points where this remarkable song needs

Early promise: This newspaper photograph from 1960 shows the 20-year-old Clive James, surrounded by an enthusiastic supporters club, honing his wit as literary editor of Sydney University's controversial student paper, *Honi Soit*.

Star quality: Pete Atkin (piano, vocals) on stage with his first band, the Chevrons, in 1961. At 15, Pete shared the singing – and the group's only microphone – on favourites from the Everly Brothers and Buddy Holly.

Throes of composition: Though the draft lyrics usually came first, fine-tuning and polishing was always a joint effort. Many of the songs were edited, amended or radically reshaped as Clive and Pete grappled with the challenge of fitting words and music together.

Creative hothouse: After Cambridge, Pete and Clive shared a flat in Swiss Cottage and then this rented house in unfashionable Gibson Square, Islington. Terraced properties in the square, which has beautiful gardens and a mock classical temple, now change hands for over £2 million, but there is no blue plaque.

First outing: Pete's solo debut, playing to a modest crowd of forty people at a Further Education College in Sittingbourne, Kent, in 1969, marked the beginning of a career lasting nearly half a century. 'I never really meant to be a performer,' he said later.

Building an image: Islington's local car-breaker's yard formed the moody backdrop for an early publicity shot. Clive experimented with a number of provocatively stylish beards as he began to build his TV career, starting with Granada's *Cinema* review show, where he took over the chair vacated by Michael Parkinson.

A King at Nightfall: The third commercial album showed the Atkin/James partnership at its best, with songs like 'Carnations on the Roof', 'Screen-Freak' and 'Thirty Year Man'. 'I should have spent RCA's money more freely, like everyone else did, and gone for a big, expensive sound,' says Pete.

Capital Radio: While Pete and his touring band played their songs for Sarah Ward's dedicated audience of insomniacs and minicab drivers, Clive sat scribbling in the corner of Capital's Studio 4 all night, working on a new idea that eventually became the much-loved 'Sessionman's Blues'.

Together at last, again: Thirty years after their last tours together, Pete and Clive were back on the road in the early 2000s, with a show that featured songs, readings and some unexpected vocal duets. 'Clive could sing in tune,' says Pete. 'But he's impetuous. He always wanted to come in too soon.'

Mutual respect: Lofty ambitions and low jokes have fuelled a lifelong songwriting partnership. 'When I met Pete, I knew I'd found my musician,' says Clive. 'He's a mighty intellect,' says Pete, 'The most talented person I have ever met.'

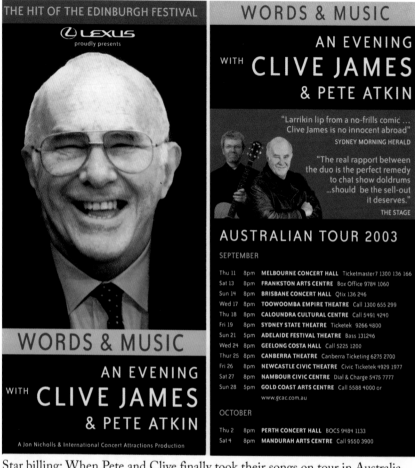

Star billing: When Pete and Clive finally took their songs on tour in Australia, they were treated like royalty, travelling in chauffeur-driven luxury with five-star hotels at every stop. Earlier tours in the UK had mainly involved dingy B&Bs and bleak rooms in Travelodges. 'That'll do me,' Clive would say. 'I could sit here for a month and write a book. It's got everything I want.'

Their names in lights: Two thousand fans packed Sydney's State Theatre for the biggest concert of the duo's Australian tour. 'People were crying with laughter,' says Pete. 'But, to be fair, that was mostly during the funny songs and when Clive read scenes from his *Unreliable Memoirs*.'

The last gig so far: Pete on stage at Walthamstow Folk Club, in November 2015, a few weeks before his near-fatal accident. The guitar is Pete's beloved black Atkin SJ. It was made for him by Alister Atkin of Canterbury, but extensive research has failed to uncover any family link between the two Atkins.

The final curtain: After nearly fifty years and two hundred remarkable and distinctive songs, the Atkin/James writing partnership still remains one of the British music industry's best-kept secrets. 'This is the work I'm known least for, but which is closest to my heart,' says Clive.

some specific updating for modern readers. While the overblown Austin Princess was strongly associated with undertakers in the 1970s, it means nothing now. And the solid, stolid, aldermanic Humber Hawks lined up behind it have also been lost, unlamented, to the march of history.

For 21st-century audiences, something of the poetic effect that Clive sought can be achieved by mentally updating the automobile references in the chorus. When you're listening to the song, just try substituting 'limos' and 'black Mercedes' at the appropriate points and you'll be fine.

> Though he had no great gifts of personality or mind
> He was generally respected, and the proof
> Was a line of hired *limos* tagging quietly behind
> A fat *black Mercedes* with carnations on the roof

But it is when the service is over and the body is to be burned that this song unveils its most startling and potent image. Because of the metal filings impregnated into the man's knuckles, he takes a little of his work with him when he goes. The hands, crossed on his chest, are described as flaring brightly 'for a Technicolor second, as he rolled into the flame'.

The notion that the work penetrates the man is as old as the hills. What you do is what you are. Shakespeare used the same idea metaphorically in his Sonnet 111, when he wrote 'My nature is subdued / To what it works in, like the dyer's hand.' But Clive's dazzling pyrotechnic image takes this a stage further. The hands, incandescent, throwing off sparks of different colours (orange for iron, white for aluminium, blue for copper) like a celebratory firework, ensure this uncelebrated man gets a spectacular send-off. It's not seen by anyone, of course. The lyrics of this song take you inside the combustion chamber to witness something no-one will ever see. But it's a picture that's hard to forget.

Clive's own social and political liberalism, as well as his own experience of factory work, informs this song. He has said many times that the Aussie 'fair go' principle is a keystone of his political beliefs. But writing 'A fair day's wage for a fair day's work is at the basis of all dignity' does not have the same effect on your audience as launching a set of images, memorably embedded in an attractively hummable song, that people will carry round with them for years to come.

Poetry does this. It makes thoughts memorable. Its shapes and sounds and heightened use of language bring ideas back to mind, often unbidden, sometimes unwanted – from Eliot's coffee spoons to Wordsworth's daffodils and Owen's gas-choked soldiers, from Hamlet's wavering to the Light Brigade's idiotic bravery, Carroll's Jabberwock and Larkin's up-fucking parents. Even those who think they know no poetry own a vast stock of phrases and images, dormant in the brain, just waiting to be recalled.

But songs, for most of us who've grown up in the second half of the 20th century – in the era before sound started to give way to vision as the staple of our daily stimulus and entertainments – do it even more than poetry. We may have access to hundreds, even thousands, of remembered and half-remembered poetic references, but that's nothing compared with what songs have done to us.

We hold millions of words and tunes in our heads. And it's that magic mnemonic power of the song that plants them there and makes them stay for ever. The words remind us of the tune and the tune reminds us of the words. That gives the songwriters an unfair advantage straight away. But then the words and the tune combine to remind us of a person, a place or a moment and we realise that half the filestore of our life's memories is indexed by songs.

In *Private Lives*, Noël Coward gave the heroine, Amanda, his famous remark 'Extraordinary how potent cheap music is'. But it was an earlier Coward play, *Hay Fever*, that first touched on the idea, in a superbly knowing snatch of dialogue. 'Are you susceptible to music?' the woman asks the man. 'I'm afraid I don't know very much about it,' he says. 'You probably are, then,' she replies.

So are we all. Music has a direct line to the unconscious. When it's combined with memorable words, it sticks for decades, sometimes for ever.

Coward suffered from the same problem as the polymathic and industrious Clive James. He did too much. As a writer, composer, lyricist, singer, actor and director, he was fated to be underrated in each of these fields. And he, too, was sometimes unaware of where and how a particular idea should be fitted in.

In the case of 'Carnations on the Roof', Clive thought, at first, that he was writing a poem. The theme had come to him while he was doing his own stint at the sheet metal factory, but it was years before he nailed it down.

'I didn't realise until later that it had to be a song lyric,' he says. When that realisation came and he worked on it with Pete Atkin, the result was one of their finest creations. The strict ABABB rhyme scheme lent itself to a driving, factory-like rhythm that quickly led Pete into thinking about the similarly harsh metal-bashing environment that had spawned Detroit's Tamla Motown tradition.

Smokey Robinson, Motown's presiding genius, had proved, time and again, that smart wordplay and long lines with complicated syntax were no bar to popular success if the music was strong enough. Several of his songs, like 'What's So Good About Goodbye?' and 'I Second That Emotion', were built around bold puns, and his ability to handle complex, conversational sentence structures has always been a key part of his writing. 'The Love I Saw in You Was Just a Mirage' and his greatest song, 'Tracks of My Tears', are minor miracles of syntactical engineering, and the fact that that's the last thing you notice about them only underlines the man's effortless skill. The second verse of 'Tracks of My Tears', for example, consists of two 30-word sentences, spread over nine lines. But the words are perfect. The long, slightly disjointed sentences reflect the way people speak, and the lyric 'sits on the row of notes', to use Clive's phrase, in a way that seems completely natural and unforced.

Once Pete had settled on the unlikely idea of setting Clive's words to 'Carnations on the Roof' to a Motown-flavoured backing, the rest flowed easily. With a line-up of top session men, led by Chris Spedding's insistent and inventive guitar, and a six-piece string section playing Pete's convincingly Temptations-like arrangement, the song blossomed into a highly plausible commercial release. Everyone who heard it believed in its potential and in March 1973, RCA put it out, backed by 'Screen-Freak', as the first Pete Atkin single for three years. The early response was good and it was played several times by Noel Edmonds on his Sunday morning show on Radio One, but nothing much happened. It crept into a few receptive ears (New Order drummer Steve Morris drew *Guardian* readers' attention to it more than thirty years later), but, yet again, the break-through to a mass audience failed to occur. Even now, though, 'Carnations on the Roof' remains one of the most flawless and com-pelling of the Atkin/James songs, a favourite in live performance and a stunning example of what the partnership could produce within the discipline of a tight set of conventions and the constraints of a three-and-a-half minute commercial single.

Carnations on the Roof

WORDS BY CLIVE JAMES, MUSIC BY PETE ATKIN

He worked setting tools for a multi-purpose punch
In a shop that made holes in steel plates.
He could hear himself think, through a fifty-minute lunch,
Of the kids, gas and stoppages, the upkeep and the rates,
While he talked about Everton and Chelsea with his mates

With gauge and micrometer, with level and with rule,
While chuck and punch were pulsing like a drum,
He checked the finished product like a master after school.
The slugs looked like money and the cutting-oil like scum
And to talk with a machinist he made signals like the dumb

Though he had no great gifts of personality or mind,
He was generally respected, and the proof
Was a line of hired Humbers tagging quietly behind
A fat Austin Princess with carnations on the roof

Forty years of metal tend to get into your skin,
The surest coin you take home from your wage.
The green cleaning-jelly only goes to rub it in
And that glitter in the wrinkle of your knuckle shows your age
Began when the dignity of work was still the rage

He was used and discarded in a game he didn't own,
But when the moment of destruction came,
He showed that a working man is more than flesh and bone.
The hands on his chest flared more brightly than his name
For a Technicolor second, as he rolled into the flame

Though he had no great gifts of personality or mind,
He was generally respected, and the proof
Was a line of hired Humbers tagging quietly behind
A fat Austin Princess with carnations on the roof

13

Who Are These People?

The trouble with Shakespeare, someone once wrote, is that it's all quotes. And the same accusation has sometimes been made about Clive James's lyrics.

On one level, it's immediately obvious, in many of the more serious songs, that Clive finds it hard to resist grabbing what he can from literary history and using it for his own ends. There are quotes and references scattered through his lyrics, and there is a small group of ardent fans out there who take a nerdy delight in spotting these borrowings – from Shakespeare himself and Donne and Blake, from Dante, Ronsard and Rilke, and from Keats and Yeats and Eliot. It would be cruel to deny them their pleasure, but for most listeners to the songs, the literary references are neither here nor there. The ones you recognise, you take for granted. And the ones you don't are generally taken as evidence that Clive has read and remembered more than everyone else and can't bear not to tell you. It's a habit that's harmless enough in itself, and the skill with which they are worked into the lyrics disarms all but the sourest critics.

What is remarkable, though, is Clive's capacity for minting an original phrase that rings and shines like some well-honed quote you feel you must have read before. In 'The Hypertension Kid', he's at his most profligate, spinning out line after line of extraordinary imagery and dazzling verbal ingenuity like a giant Catherine wheel. Yet these are delivered within the discipline of a strict metre and rhyme scheme and the requirement to achieve a genuinely conversational tone.

Early on in the song, we have no idea who the Hypertension Kid is. But the exchanges are brisk, colloquial and glittering. 'It's my lousy memory,' the narrator tells the Kid. 'What other men forget I still remember.' That's dialogue that would stand out in any stage play. But two can play at that game. When it's the Kid's turn to speak, his advice is couched in equally witty and unexpected terms. 'The slide from grace is really more like gliding, / And I've found the trick is not to stop the sliding / But to find a graceful way of staying slid.'

The punchlines come thick and fast. 'The flies are still alive inside the amber' brings the response 'Your metaphors are murder'. But it's not all verbal swordplay; the Kid has practical wisdom to offer. Like Confucius, he believes in bending with the wind. 'I know the mood – give in to it a little. / The man who shatters is the man who's brittle. / Lay off the brakes and steer into the skid.' And the Kid, whoever he is, recommends taking a philosophical view of one's own lapses. Keep it all in perspective, he advises, and don't beat yourself up.

'For evil' said the Hypertension Kid,
'Is better contemplated in the deeds of others,
Mass-murderers and men who knife their mothers.
Be glad that what you've done is all you did'

This is Clive at his most beguiling – witty, streetwise and sardonic, but with something interesting to say that goes far beyond the context of the song.

The tune that Pete came up with matches these lyrics artfully, driving the song along at a brisk pace, but never getting in the way of the remarkable words. The original arrangement, on *A King at Nightfall*, is tense and edgily neurotic, with a thudding, insistent fuzz rhythm guitar that ends in an anguished wail of feedback. But it is the radical reworking of the same materials on *Midnight Voices*, the 'greatest hits' album of remakes that came out in 2007, that really brings out the depth and subtleties of the song. The vocals are slower, cooler, almost languid in places, leaving more room to savour the words and handling the big reveal in the last verse far better. As both characters turn to leave, one towards the street, the other disappearing into the mirror behind the bar, the audience's suspicions are confirmed. 'My second self,' the line is almost thrown away, 'the Hypertension Kid.' And it's all the better for being played down. This is Pete Atkin at his best, trusting in the power of the words and using the music, in a gently ironic way, to bring out their quality without amplifying them unnecessarily.

It has always been a joke between the two of them that Pete liked the lyrics of 'The Hypertension Kid' more than Clive did. Clive would deny, with little credibility, that he knew who the characters in the song were. Pete said he did, and that he knew them well, and that he still liked them anyway.

The Hypertension Kid

WORDS BY CLIVE JAMES, MUSIC BY PETE ATKIN

Last night I met the Hypertension Kid,
Grimly chasing shorts with halves of bitter
In a Mayfair club they call the Early Quitter.
He met my eyes and hit me for a quid

'I spend fortunes in this rat-trap,' said the Kid.
'But the plush and flock soak up the brain's kerfuffle
And I like to see a servile barman shuffle.
If sympathy's your need, let's hear your bid'

'It's my lousy memory,' I told the Kid.
'What other men forget I still remember.
The flies are still alive inside the amber.
It's a garbage can with rubbish for a lid'

'Your metaphors are murder,' said the Kid.
'I know the mood – give in to it a little.
The man who shatters is the man who's brittle.
Lay off the brakes and steer into the skid'

'Strained virtue warps the soul,' announced the Kid.
'Those forced attempts at cleanliness that linger
Like soap between your wedding ring and finger.
They're residues of which you're better rid'

WHO ARE THESE PEOPLE?

'For evil' said the Hypertension Kid,
'Is better contemplated in the deeds of others,
Mass-murderers and men who knife their mothers.
Be glad that what you've done is all you did'

'With me, the problem's women,' said the Kid.
'Befuddled, fondled under separate covers,
One and all they've gone to other lovers,
As I powered down to zero from the grid'

'But I love the little darlings,' sighed the Kid.
'The slide from grace is really more like gliding,
And I've found the trick is not to stop the sliding
But to find a graceful way of staying slid'

'As for the dreadful memories,' said the Kid,
'The waste and poison in the spirit's river,
Relax your hands and let the bastards quiver.
They tremble more the more you keep it hid'

We turned to leave the bar, me and the Kid,
I, with lightened head and lessened terror,
Toward the street, and he into the mirror,
My second self, the Hypertension Kid

14

All the Dead Were Strangers

'I met my buddy Kovacs, stripping down his M16. He said, "I think the barrel got hot – know what I mean?"…'

Alongside the tales of love and longing, guilt and ecstasy, music and existential melancholy, alongside the whimsy and the satire, the humour and the flashing wit, there are some songs in the Atkin/James canon that insist on being taken utterly seriously. Clive and Pete can do brutal – and they can do it with gritty, unsentimental power.

'All the Dead Were Strangers' was written during the Vietnam War and triggered by the notorious My Lai massacre, in which more than 400 unarmed men, women and children were slaughtered by a small unit of US Army troops. The massacre was covered up for eighteen months before the press got hold of the story in 1969. As the details emerged of gang-raped women, bayoneted children and a brief, crazed orgy of destruction that included burning homes to the ground, poisoning wells and shooting farm animals, My Lai helped harden the opposition to the war. It also helped change people's views of the armies involved.

Instead of being seen in glorified terms as bold, brave men, marching proudly to war to save the world and stem the spread of

Communism in Southeast Asia, the 'grunts', the front-line soldiers, began to be recognised as victims of their deluded political masters. As America's sons came home in body bags and returning veterans told their tales of mad, gung-ho generals and frightened, alienated, drug-addled conscripts, public attitudes turned. The young Americans and Australians who'd come to London and Paris and Stockholm were no longer talked about as cowardly draft-dodgers, even by politicians on this side of the world. The nightmare of 'Nam dragged on for several more years, with the last US troops finally leaving in August 1973. But long before the end, everyone knew it had all been a ghastly and costly aberration.

The war in Vietnam inspired many great pop, rock and folk songs, from Barry McGuire's 'Eve of Destruction' to Country Joe and the Fish's 'I-Feel-Like-I'm-Fixing-to-Die Rag' ('And it's 1, 2, 3…'), and from Jimmy Cliff's 'Vietnam' to Lennon's 'Imagine' and 'Happy Xmas (War Is Over)' and Marvin Gaye's 'What's Goin' On?'. It also inspired many more songs long after the event, but those must be seen as a different category. What is interesting about the contemporary Vietnam songs is the number of different approaches the songwriters took – jauntily sarcastic, in the case of Country Joe, directly political ('Eve of Destruction' famously pointed out that kids too young to vote were deemed old enough to kill, and, of course, to die) or less specific, as in John Lennon's anti-war classics. But very few songs actually took a documentary approach, launching the listener into the middle of the battlefield.

'All the Dead Were Strangers' takes you there, in a way that is graphic, cinematic and chillingly credible. Kovacs is smiling, but his eyes are dead. Polonsky has looted a transistor radio from a dead gook. When his buddy protests ('We weren't sent in here to steal'), he responds with a threatening snarl: 'Stow it! How do you know what I feel? What the hell else is there in this for me?'

Kovacs is no saint. The overheated barrel of his M16 got that way from a busy morning's murdering. Logically, it makes no difference to the dead if their few possessions are taken as the spoils of war. Yet there's still a residual glimmer of decency that makes him object to Polonsky's theft. These kids are young, confused, conflicted and trau-matised – and totally out of their depth in the hellish chaos they create.

The vision is detailed and horrific. We see the 'ladies so old they hardly bled', the kids 'who never needed a red hole in the head', the gunships that 'hose the ruins, for reasons hell knows why' and the way the narrator, no hero himself, turns in vain to drugs to ease the pain of the nightmare. 'All the Dead Were Strangers' does, in a single, memorable four-and-a-half minute song, much of what films like *Apocalypse Now*, *The Deer Hunter*, *Platoon* and *Full Metal Jacket* did, much later, with the full resources of Hollywood at their disposal.

At the core of all this is the disorientating, dehumanising effect of modern warfare. The dead really are total strangers. A few hours earlier, the GIs didn't know their village existed. The troops are dropped in by the 'birds' (the helicopters) early in the morning, slaughter the civilians and burn their homes to the ground and then wait to be lifted out again, job done. The narrator is shocked by the bloody arbitrariness of what he's involved in, but he's more bemused than angry. As the gunships arrive overhead to strafe the devastated village, he asks plaintively: 'Why bother? Why bother all the dead?'

Pete's music for this awe-inspiring song is calm, almost pretty, and deceptively original.

'Secretly, I've always liked the way the harmonies move,' he says, 'with that little out-of-rhythm twiddle on the D minor, and each verse ending up in F so that it needs a key change up to G to start the new verse. I don't know why I haven't used that idea again.'

But it's not about the technicalities. It's about pitching it at the right level, getting the pacing right and resisting the temptation to pump up the emotion, except in the anguished repetition of 'All the dead were, all the dead were, all the dead were, all the dead were strangers' at the end of each verse. On the previous album, there might have been jagged, distorted guitars to emphasise the violence. Here, on *A King at Nightfall*, there is a simple, restrained arrangement, with subtle piano and guitar fills and a rather matter-of-fact story-telling vocal from Pete. The result is a stunningly effective marriage of words and music – and a vivid illustration of Clive's often-stated belief that songs should be able to tackle any subject under the sun, shining light on every aspect of human experience in the same way that prose and poetry can.

Over the years, 'All the Dead Were Strangers' has managed to be ignored even more comprehensively than the other great Atkin/James songs. It has often been omitted from the set list for live gigs, presumably on the grounds that it won't necessarily make for a fun evening. But when it is performed, the effect on audiences is striking. People listen with rapt attention. They don't cough or shift in their seats. You can see that they're thinking, not just about Vietnam, but about Afghanistan, Iraq and Syria, too, and all the messy, savage, complicated and pointless wars that litter today's world. And I have never seen an audience that hasn't erupted afterwards in a wave of applause. It's not one of Clive and Pete's most engaging songs – in a poll of Atkin/James favourites on *Midnight Voices*, the long-running online fan forum, 'All the Dead Were Strangers' didn't even make the Top 50 – but it's surely one of their most complete and impressive achievements.

All the Dead Were Strangers

WORDS BY CLIVE JAMES, MUSIC BY PETE ATKIN

I met my buddy Kovacs, stripping down his M16.
He said 'I think the barrel got hot — know what I mean?'
And his smiling mouth looked friendly
But his eyes, like all the dead, were strangers.
All the dead were strangers

Just lying there were ladies so old they hardly bled.
Thin kids who never needed a red hole in the head.
We were all in this together.
We were friends, but all the dead were strangers.
All the dead were strangers

We bumped into Polonsky, and Polonsky hollered 'Look!
It's a Japanese transistor I swiped off of a gook
And it don't even have no batteries.'
And he laughed that all the dead were strangers.
All the dead were strangers

Kovacs said 'You crumb-dumb, we weren't sent in here to steal.'
And Polonsky answered 'Stow it! How do you know what I feel?
What the hell else is there in this
For me? Like, all the dead were strangers.'
All the dead were strangers

I left them two to argue and I walked between the huts.
It's a bad day when a king-hit of grass won't calm your guts,
But it helps you to remember,
Or forget, that all the dead were strangers.
All the dead were strangers

The birds that lift us in here lift us out through the same sky
And the gunships hose the ruins for reasons hell knows why.
And I can only yell 'Why bother?
Why bother all the dead?' They were strangers.
All the dead were strangers

15

Memento Mori

The hit songs of the 1920s, 1930s and 1940s, the classics that form the Great American Songbook, were often not as we remember them. Where most popular songs of the last sixty years have been built around a verse, a chorus and a middle eight, many of the earlier songs – in fact, most of the finest efforts from the Gershwins, Berlins, Porters and Kerns of this world – were written as show tunes. Many of them, including standards like Porter's 'Night and Day' and Gershwin's 'The Man I Love', had slow, half-spoken and now largely forgotten introductions that rambled on at some length before the real song got going. Irving Berlin's 'What'll I Do?', for example, has one of these introductory or 'sectional' verses, muttering along for sixteen bars about the romance divine (''tis broken and cannot be mended'), like some dull sub-operatic recitative, before the familiar and brilliantly simple melody begins.

Pete's setting of Clive's lyrics for 'Senior Citizens' draws on this tradition in an unusual way. The long introductory verse paints a cold, unflinching picture of old age ('The drying spine that bends them to the ground / The way their ankles fold over their shoes'), half-sung, half-spoken, and full of fresh and unexpected ideas and imagery. The neat dexterity of lines like 'They've lost touch with the touch of other hands / That once came to caress and then to help' is chillingly evocative, while even Clive's inventive wordplay is kept firmly under control. 'They've had their day, and half of the day after' adds a new twist to an old cliché, without drawing attention to itself. But the real surprise comes when the introduction ends and the song breaks into a more relaxed, melodic mode.

Although the chords – and even the actual notes of the melody – remain the same as those used for the bleak introduction, the tune that emerges in the verse is warm, romantic and hard to forget. Stretched across the long, irregular lines of the intro, it didn't seem to add up to much. Tightened up across these shorter lines, it shifts into sharp focus. It's one of Pete's most poignant, lyrical melodies – and, of course, its comfortable hummability is predictably deceptive. We're back with the young now, full of confidence and potential and eager for the love the old have left behind. 'It's so simple, when it's you, for me to coax from my guitar / The usual on how fine you are / Like this calm night, like that bright star' Pete sings. And it's only elliptically, in the last four lines, that the connection is made between the cocksure optimism of youth and the dark, demeaning inevitability of age: 'The sands will take so long to fall / The neck so slim, the glass so tall.'

'It's a miracle, singing that song,' says Pete. 'It's a fabulous piece of lyric writing. It sounds like a conventional love song, and then, at the end, the chill of the punchline is just stunning. I still love singing it, because I love the effect it has on people – the way they're shocked and surprised by it. I have to choose my moments to sing it, as it's a song that needs the audience to be listening. But it's Clive at his best, and that's as good as anybody.'

Pete always introduces 'Senior Citizens' rather innocently, as if it's going to be just another song about the old – a simple picture, from a safe distance, of the infirmities and indignities of age.

'But audiences don't know what they're in for. You get those brutally realistic images, in the introductory verse, of the old people just crumbling, and then it breaks into the sweet simplicity of the love song. And then, suddenly, Clive ties it all back together in the ending, joining the dots and making the connection along the path that everyone in the room is going to travel. "We're never going to be like that." "Oh yes, you are." It's fantastic.'

Having achieved their own senior citizenship, to their evident surprise, Clive and Pete found that they still had things to say and songs to write. Their final album, *The Colours of the Night*, was released quite recently, in July 2015. Several of the songs touch on end-of-life issues, including 'You Better Face It Boy', 'Slow Down For Me' and the last track of the last album, 'Me To Thank' (which, incidentally, uses a free-form, out-of-tempo introductory verse, like 'Senior Citizens', though there's no lilting chorus to follow it – in fact, as Pete comments, 'There's nothing to follow'). These are all fine songs, but none of them has quite the subtle insight and graphic impact of 'Senior Citizens'. The surprise is, in retrospect, that this masterpiece was created back in 1973, by two young songwriters with a combined age of 60. They wouldn't have made one pensioner between them. Like Lennon, at 24, writing his brilliantly empathetic song about needing the help that he never needed when he was 'younger, so much younger than today', this is a reminder that songwriting is not documentary-making. It is the work of the imagination, and it can sometimes rise to great heights.

Senior Citizens

WORDS BY CLIVE JAMES, MUSIC BY PETE ATKIN

You've seen the way they get around
With nothing beyond burdens left to lose.
The drying spine that bends them near the ground,
The way their ankles fold over their shoes.
They've had their day and half of the day after
And all the shares they ever held in laughter
Are now just so many old engravings.
Their sands have run out long before their savings,
And the fun ran out so long before the sands.

They've lost touch with the touch of other hands
That once came to caress and then to help.
A single tumble means a broken hip.
The hair grows thinner on the scalp
And thicker on the upper lip.
And who is there to care, or left to please?

It's so easy, when we're young,
For me to wield a silver tongue
And cleverly place you among
The girls the boys have always sung

It's so simple, when it's you,
For me to coax from my guitar

The usual on how fine you are,
Like this calm night, like that bright star

And the rest would follow on.
The rest would follow on

And there'll be time to try it all.
I'm sure the thrill will never pall.
The sand will take so long to fall.
The neck so slim, the glass so tall

16

Sessionman's Blues

Several months after our night with Sarah Ward at Capital Radio, Clive was back there again for another all-night session, this time with Pete and the three-piece backing band, Mama Flyer, that he'd worked with on the promotional tour for *The Road of Silk*. As a tour, that had been a great success, the heavier rock sound going down well with the student-dominated audiences. As a promotion, it was a disaster. It sparked plenty of demand for the album, but there were no LPs in the shops when the customers came in. RCA had assumed Pete was a minority taste and had only pressed 5000 copies. When the shortfall became obvious, early on in the tour, RCA executives promised to press more immediately. But it didn't happen.

'The album sold out everywhere in the first week,' says Pete. 'So we were doing 26 gigs in 31 days and there was nothing in the shops to back us up. I was furious. I complained to RCA and they promised it would never happen again. And then it did, of course, the following year. I went on the road again, with a different band, to promote *Secret Drinker*, and the same thing happened. Sold out in a week and no more albums for people to buy. The RCA pressing plant in County Durham was busy churning out copies of the new Bowie album,

Elvis Presley and some big posthumous Jim Reeves hit and they weren't going to stop all that to press more of *Secret Drinker*.'

In Capital Radio's Studio 4 that night, in April 1974, Pete and the band were on top form. Clive talked about Britain and Australia, TV and films, poetry and music. Pete sang and talked to Sarah about how the songs came to be written. But Clive, the man who never stops working, had something else on his mind. As the night went by, he could be seen bent over his notebook. And by the end of the programme, he was ready to reveal what he'd been doing.

He'd had an idea for a song, during the first hour of the programme, and had been writing and rewriting it whenever the music was being played, right through the early hours of the morning. As the show came to an end, he read out what he'd been working on, the complete lyric for 'Sessionman's Blues'.

Session men were the backbone of the music industry in the Sixties and Seventies. They were the hired hands who could be brought in at short notice to beef up any recording session, usually playing at fixed minimum rates set by the Musicians' Union, shuffling between studios and often, as the song says, working on two, three or even four albums in a single day. A few, like guitarist Jimmy Page and bassist John Paul Jones (who later got together and formed Led Zeppelin) and keyboard players Billy Preston (who played with the Beatles on the *Let It Be* sessions) and Rick Wakeman, went on to become rich and famous in their own right. Most, despite their phenomenal skills and versatility, remained firmly in the shadows, making a steady income and only showing up in the small print of an album's track listings.

A good session man would usually have great sightreading skills and be able to switch between styles quickly and effortlessly, jumping from pop to rock to country, funk, jazz or folk styles at the drop of a hat. There'd be a click on the talkback after a take and a brief comment from the producer in the control room ('That's great, Jimmy, but could you give it more of a Motown feel?') and they'd go again, sometimes changing the whole style of a track two or three times in an hour. Many session men could walk into a studio, read the dots and play a part note-perfect first time round, often allowing the producer and recording engineers to get what they needed in just a handful of takes. Professionalism was taken for granted and the top session musicians were held in awed respect by the stars they backed.

Pete and Clive had seen the nonchalant brilliance of some of the best UK session men during the making of the second Pete Atkin LP, *Driving Through Mythical America*, a much heavier, more confident-sounding album than its predecessor. The line-up was different on each of the five main recording days, with Chris Spedding playing guitar on songs like 'Sunlight Gate' and 'Lady of a Day' and Alan Parker (who had played, uncredited, on Love Affair's big hit, 'Everlasting Love') taking over for others, such as the title track and 'No Dice'. But it hardly seemed to matter who was booked for a particular session. The skill and inventiveness of these battle-hardened musicians was a revelation.

'I remember the day we went into the studio to do "No Dice",' says Pete. 'We'd decided we wanted to record all the tracks on the albums "as live", meaning that all the musicians played simultaneously, with no overdubs, so that we'd get a proper, rich band sound. It was an important song, one of Clive's six-minute epics, and I wanted to get it right.'

'No Dice' was certainly a big, complicated song, with five lengthy verses, a three-line chorus at the end of each and words that jump-cut to four different historical death scenes, 'linking the ways men die with how they grow'. It was one of Clive's ambitious 'history songs', a group of lyrics that divides the fans more than any other. For some, these songs, including 'Search and Destroy' and 'The Last Hill That Shows You All the Valley', are among the finest of all the Atkin/James creations. For others, they teeter on a knife-edge of self-conscious artiness, occasionally lapsing into bathos. By the time we get to the final line of 'The Last Hill', for example, which talks about helicopters on the walls of Troy, Clive has lost me. To my ear, the image seems overwrought and jarring, though I have met other enthusiasts who would happily nominate this line as one of their all-time favourites.

The lyrics of 'No Dice' are more impressionistic, staying just the right side of the line and sidestepping the risks posed by this kind of anachronistic imagery. But it is still a formidably tricky song, and Pete was aware that there were plenty of pitfalls lying in wait for both the singer and the musicians.

It was a long way from simple three-chord pop, too, using a total of sixteen different chords. Just playing it right would be hard enough for the backing group of the day, which consisted of Alan Parker, Herbie Flowers (bass) and Barry Morgan (drums), all of them used to working together as members of the chart-topping Blue Mink. Adding the feel and subtleties that would differentiate the verses was likely to be even more challenging. But Pete needn't have worried.

He'd done everything he could to prepare for the recording, writing out the parts for each instrument in minute detail. But he and the band were only just starting the third verse of the first run-through when someone said 'That's fine – let's go for it.'

'What?'

'Let's go for a take.'

The tapes rolled and the entire six-minute song was done first time, in a single take.

'It's amazing, when I look back on it,' says Pete. 'They just got it in one, and they did such a good job. I love what Herbie Flowers did with the bass, starting with a simple bass line and gradually winding it up, getting more and more ambitious with each verse. And I still can't believe how great Barry Morgan's drumming is – full of crispness and flexibility, with tiny, subtle rhythmic ripples. It's so fast, and it swings so hard. It's just magic. Yet he'd never played the song before – and, of course, he never played it again.'

Listening to the track now, on *Driving Through Mythical America*, you can hear Pete's excitement as it unfolds. There is even an obvious fluff in the vocals in the third verse, where he starts the word 'chipped' with an 's' and ends up singing 'schipped'. But that one little imperfection was a small price to pay for the spontaneous energy of the band's performance and the first-take track was left undoctored in the final mix.

Watching these inspired musical mercenaries at work had made a deep impression on Clive, and it was this respect for their craftsmanship that bubbled to the surface as he sat working on his ideas for 'Sessionman's Blues' throughout the long night at Capital Radio.

What he read out over the airwaves at the end of the show wasn't a song, of course. It sounded promising, but it was still just words on a page. There were hints at the wearily matter-of-fact cynicism of a talented musician who is often hired to play rubbish ('I played what they told me to play') and may, at times, turn to the bottle for solace ('I drink a session man's booze'). There were also ringing lines that paid tribute to the session player's professionalism ('But my tenor blows what's on the chart. / A single run through and I've got the whole solo by heart'). But the most intriguing possibilities for Pete lay in the chorus that followed each of the three verses.

At the end of the first verse, the chorus of 'Sessionman's Blues' is just two lines.

I've got the Sessionman's Blues,
The Squattin'-in-a-Booth-Alone Blues

After the second verse, the chorus gains an extra line, emphasising the separateness of the sax player as he sits in the corner of the studio, hemmed in by a wall of acoustic screens, overdubbing his contribution.

I've got the Sessionman's Blues,
The Squattin'-in-a-Booth-Alone,
Isolated-Microphone Blues

For the final chorus, another extra line is added, with a reference to the welcome 25 per cent bonus payable, under Musicians' Union rules, whenever a studio musician is required to 'double' on a second instrument within a session.

I've got the Sessionman's Blues,
The Squattin'-in-a-Booth-Alone,
Isolated-Microphone,
Doubling-on-Baritone Blues

Within days of the Sarah Ward all-nighter, Pete had come up with one of his best and most memorable tunes, a gently lyrical melody line that stuck closely within the 12-bar blues tradition, offset by typically unexpected harmonic twists. 'Sessionman's Blues' ranges across sixteen different chords, rather more than many blues guitarists will use in a lifetime. Yet it seems simple, and it has that elusive earworm factor. For all the qualities of Clive's words, this is probably one of the few Atkin/James tracks that would make a successful instrumental. With the right languid clarinet or tenor taking the lead line, it could easily form the basis for something that could stand alongside Sidney Bechet or Louis Armstrong.

The original version of the song, recorded in 1974 for the *Secret Drinker* album, featured a jazzy trio of Pete's piano, double bass and drums, with a neat baritone solo by Ronnie Ross after the last chorus. In the new version on the *Midnight Voices* album, thirty-three years later, Pete sings better than before but leaves the piano to the excellent Simon Wallace. The track is lit up all the way through by lovely tenor sax from Alan Barnes, who appropriately and obligingly doubles on baritone for the final rich and surprising solo.

Long-time fans of the Atkin/James catalogue often make the mistake of trying to recruit new listeners among their friends and relations by playing them their own favourite tracks, which are often not the most accessible. 'Sessionman's Blues' isn't going to change anyone's perspectives on life, love and death, but it is a very fine song in its own right. Alongside the other classics on musical themes – 'Thief in the Night' and the tunefully melancholy 'Thirty Year Man' – it rarely fails to stir the desire to hear more.

Sessionman's Blues

WORDS BY CLIVE JAMES, MUSIC BY PETE ATKIN

I've got the Sessionman's Blues.
I've played on three albums today.
I paid a session man's dues.
I played what they told me to play,
Then I climbed in my Rover 3-litre and motored away

I've got the Sessionman's Blues,
The Squattin'-in-a-Booth-Alone Blues

I've got the Sessionman's Blues,
But I get the dots right from the start.
I drink a session man's booze,
But my tenor blows what's on the chart.
A single run through and I've got the whole solo by heart

I've got the Sessionman's Blues,

The Squattin'-in-a-Booth-Alone,

Isolated-Microphone Blues

I've got the Sessionman's Blues.

I'm booked up a lifetime ahead.

I get a session man's news.

The voice on the blower just said

They want me to work on the afternoon after I'm dead

I've got the Sessionman's Blues,

The Squattin'-in-a-Booth-Alone,

Isolated-Microphone,

Doubling-on-Baritone Blues

17

At the Back of the Horse

As the half of the Atkin/James partnership responsible for the music, Pete is used to being cast as the back end of the pantomime horse. It's been his fate for nearly fifty years. Friends of mine who have seen draft chapters of this book have already warned me not to let Clive's fame and quotability overshadow his colleague's essential contribution. 'All we are saying,' they tell me, 'is give Pete a chance.'

To some extent, it's a built-in problem. Everyone who reads this book can read, but less than a quarter of the adults in Britain can read music, even at the most basic level. My publisher tells me that printing the odd stave here and there with examples of Pete's music would actually put people off and reduce the book's readership. And there's a limit to how much you can say in words about any piece of music without drifting off into the realms of the abstract or the technical. It's like trying to describe a flavour or a perfume, or dignity or beauty. There is simply no substitute for the direct experience.

Yet the music is what hits you first when you listen to a song. Most performances and recordings begin with some kind of instrumental intro, whether it's the volley of drumbeats from Ringo that launches us into 'She Loves You' or the first thrilling riff from Clapton's guitar that introduces 'Layla'. Even if the words begin straight away – as in 'Heartbreak Hotel', 'Bohemian Rhapsody' or Kanye West's 'Good Life' – it's the sound, rather than the lyric, that makes the first impression. In the first few seconds, before you've had time to process or respond to the words, you're reacting to melody, tone and rhythm and picking up on the genre of music that's reaching your ears.

If there's one person who has never underestimated the importance of the music, it's Clive himself. 'A song should hit you in the knees first and climb to the brain later,' he said. 'I wanted the words to filter through, not leap out.'

Years later, he complained that this hadn't happened often enough in their early recordings and blamed himself for allowing many of these tracks to be mixed with the vocals too far forward, 'so the words reached the listener before the music did'. The thought occurred to him right there in the studio, he said, but, surrounded as he was by musicians and sound technicians so much better qualified to judge these things, he had bitten his lip and assumed they knew best. In his occasional moods of self-flagellation, over the decades, he blamed the prominence given to his words for Pete's lack of commercial success.

Pete doesn't see it like that. He feels the albums did their job, but he believes they could have cut through the clutter more effectively if he had insisted on a bigger sound.

'We gained enough attention for me to go on and make half a dozen albums in the Seventies, which is not nothing,' he says. 'It's easy to forget now, when anyone can do anything at home, in the back bedroom, but in those days you had to win a contract with a big record company to make an album at all. It was a big deal, which was why I was so cautious not to overspend and make any rash decisions about extravagant line-ups and productions.

'The reason an album like *The Road of Silk* sounds the way it does is because it was done for tuppence ha'penny. I didn't realise it then, but it would have made no difference to RCA if we'd spent £150,000, rather than £10,000, on the studio time and musicians we used to make the album. We could have block-booked the studio for a fortnight or three weeks and the record company wouldn't have batted an eyelid. Being overcautious was a huge mistake on my part. RCA wouldn't have minded. They didn't care. The fact that I was being economical was of no interest to them whatsoever, because they were making so many millions from Bowie and Presley and Jim Reeves. I should have spent their money and piled the resources in. God knows, there were many people who did that and never had any more success than we did. But there's always a chance, if you make this big sound that it might add the wow factor and catch people's ears and help it break through.'

From his privileged viewpoint at the back of the horse, Pete sees the commercial near-misses as probably being, in the end, to do with his music. In fact, he believes, it's always the music that decides whether a song will fire the public's imagination.

'The commercial success of a song hardly ever depends on the words,' he says. 'And it's almost never inhibited by the words, either.

'A great popular song *always* has memorable music, and *sometimes* has memorable words. But you can't get a hit with something that has terrific words but doesn't have memorable music. It always depends primarily on the music, and the way the words and the music lock together to become inseparable.'

It's this tight, interdependent relationship, linking the shapes and rhythms of the words to the drive and power of the music, that enables some of the best rock songs to carry off unexpectedly wordy, ambitious or complicated lyrics. The Kinks' 'Lola' runs to more than 300 words, a lot longer than most of Clive's 'literary' lyrics. Bruce Springsteen's 'Born To Run' is even longer. But Springsteen was quite clear about what his ambitions were. He wanted 'Born To Run' to have it all, to sound 'like Roy Orbison singing Bob Dylan, produced by Phil Spector', and he spent six months in the studio trying to make sure it did. That's six months on one song – the whole album took well over a year. When it came to spending the record company's money on what was, for him, a last-chance effort to make a commercially successful album, The Boss was ruthless and unhesitating. Meanwhile, at exactly the same time, back in Rockfield Studios, Monmouth, and London's Morgan Studios, Pete was recording and mixing the last of the RCA albums, *Live Libel*, in ten days flat.

Whether a Phil Spector Wall of Sound production would have made the difference and propelled Pete and Clive's songs into the pop mainstream is an open question. But there's no doubt that having any kind of hit, either with Pete's recordings or via a cover version by some better-known artist, would have made people look at all their other songs in a different way. And it must have occurred to them many times that writing something simple and elemental – a 'Wild Thing' or a 'Twist and Shout' – would change their prospects for ever.

'I don't think Clive could have brought himself to do that,' says Pete. 'He's clever enough, of course – clever enough to do almost anything he set out to do. But I don't think he'd ever have been able to sit down and write "Wild Thing". Strange as it may seem, though, I think maybe I could have done it. I think Clive knew that, and that may be what's there in the back of his mind when he talks about his inhibiting effect on my commercial musical career.'

If the idea of Pete Atkin turning his talents to the task of writing something so basic seems farfetched, it's worth remembering that 'Wild Thing' itself wasn't written by some Neanderthal musical primitive sitting outside a cave and banging out the chords on a guitar strung with woolly mammoth sinews. Although it was mis-credited to the lead singer of The Troggs, Reg Presley, on the group's original Atco label pressing, it was actually composed to order by Chip Taylor, who had been asked by a New York record producer to come up with a commercial single for a band called The Wild Ones. Taylor was an accomplished songwriter who normally wrote 'pretty little country songs', and he described the process of creating 'Wild Thing' as just 'chugging away on a couple of chords' until he stumbled on something 'sexy, cool and sweaty'. The composer, brother of actor Jon Voight and Angelina Jolie's uncle, never wrote anything else remotely like it, though he had many more hits with songs like 'Angel of the Morning' and Janis Joplin's 'Try (Just a Little Bit Harder)', before leaving the music business behind, turning to the blackjack tables and reinventing himself as a professional gambler.

Pete's feeling that he just might have been able to write an out-and-out commercial hit was never tested, though the last – and probably least impressive – of the duo's 1970s records, *Live Libel*, does go some way to support his view. Billed as 'an album of musical tributes to insufficiently neglected contemporary artists', it was dashed off more or less under protest to fulfil the terms of the RCA contract and was largely made up of parodies of current pop styles. These songs had proved very useful at live gigs, where their easy accessibility and satirical caricatures of artists ranging from Kris Kristofferson to Leonard Cohen could be deployed to give audiences a breathing space between the more important, and more challenging, numbers. Piled in together on a single album, they simply didn't work.

'It was always handy to be able to pull one of those out of the bag in a club or college gig, just to perk up an audience's attention,' says Pete. 'It would give people a chance to relax and laugh along for a couple of minutes, and then they'd be happy to sit still and listen to something serious like "Driving Through Mythical America", "All the Dead Were Strangers" or "Senior Citizens".

'But we shouldn't have put them on an LP. I regret that now, because we already had a lot of material we were very proud of lined up for the next album and it never got made. Those new songs remained unheard, except at gigs, for twenty-five years, until we eventually recorded them on our own low-budget do-it-yourself double album, *The Lakeside Sessions* in 2001.'

What the parodies on *Live Libel* did prove, though, was that Pete could write music in many popular styles that were not recognisably his own. Taken individually, many of the songs had something to offer, both musically and lyrically. The Kristofferson piss-take, 'Song for Rita', didn't just mock his sentimental delivery. It also included some delicately barbed lines that bore the unmistakeable stamp of the Clive James wit.

The way my arms around you touch the centre of my being,
As I step inside the marshland of your mind,
Makes me weak inside my senses, like a dog hit by a diesel
And more alone than Milton goin' blind

And I know I need to lose you if I ever want to find you
'Cause the poet's way is finished from the start.
And I feel a palpitation kinda flutter in my forehead
As I think the problem over in my heart

Yes, I guess I'll always never know the question to your answer,
If I can't be doin' wrong by feelin' right.
But I'm really lookin' forward to how you'll be lookin' backward
When I'm walkin' with you sideways through the night

Not great art, perhaps, but pretty clever, in a smartypants kind of way. And 'Black Funk Rex', 'Rattlesnake Rock' and the cod James Taylor song, 'Sheer Quivering Genius', all showed previously unsuspected aspects of Pete's musical ability, hitting their targets squarely on the nose. He's uncomfortable now, though, about the air of supercilious smugness that he sees pervading the album. The songs may have been intended as fairly affectionate parodies, but it's hard to tickle someone with a scalpel.

'Those songs,' he says. 'There's a snootiness about them that I really don't like. There's a sniffy, we're-better-than-those-idiots superiority. I think it laid us open to the suspicion that we were actually jealous of the artists we mocked, on the unworthy grounds that anyone who made money – just like we so consistently didn't – must automatically be second-rate.'

The best of these songs, from an outsider's point of view, is 'Stranger in Town', which is based on a sustained inversion of every traditional country cliché. Beginning with the rousing couplet 'I never will remember how that stranger came to town / He walked in without a swagger, got a job and settled down', it builds neatly, over the last three verses, to an unexpected pinnacle of bathos.

> From Kansas to Wyoming, from Contention to Cheyenne,
> His name meant less than nothing and it didn't scare a man.
> So folks didn't worship him or fear him
> And I can't remember ever going near him
>
> He didn't tote a shotgun with the barrels both sawn off,
> So people didn't hit the deck or dive behind a trough.
> He walked the street in silence, ignored on every side,
> And it's doubtful if he could even ride
>
> I never could remember how that stranger met his death.
> He was absolutely senile, and with his dying breath,
> He forgot to ask his womenfolk to kiss him.
> And afterwards they didn't even miss him

This isn't snide sniping at the idols of the day. It's a proper idea, cleverly executed, and, as a result, it holds up well, even forty years on, despite an arrangement that trembles on the brink of Bonzonian lunacy.

All composing, of course, like all writing, is pastiche. It's how you do it that counts, and whether you can add the spark of energy that makes the monster come to life. In creating the music that frames Clive's lyrics, Pete has done this time and time again, drawing on a vast reservoir of musical knowledge, styles and influences. But his chameleon-like ability to match the music to the words is a double-edged sword. It makes it hard to talk, in general terms, about a Pete Atkin style, though anyone familiar with the songs knows perfectly well that there is something quite distinctively Pete about almost all his tunes.

The melody will often take an unexpected turn, sometimes at the risk of wrongfooting the listener. And the chords – so often the starting point for a successful pop song – invariably come after the melody.

'I can honestly say I've never started out from or with a chord sequence,' says Pete. 'The tempo is always the first thing I need to find. After that, the harmonies I hear in my head derive first from the melody and second from a perverse desire to avoid doing anything too obvious. I never saw the point of doing again what other people were already doing well.'

It's quite possible that Pete and Clive could have achieved more success, in purely commercial terms, if they had not teamed up together. If Pete had collaborated with a more ordinary, or at least less extraordinary, lyricist, he'd have been working on a smaller canvas, but he might have been encouraged to let his music take centre stage more often. If Clive had had a songwriting partner without Pete's accommodating flexibility and ingenuity, he'd probably have been forced to write less ambitious, more easily accessible lyrics and keep his most extravagant conceits and imagery for his poetry. But who could have wished that on them?

If even the very earliest Atkin/James songs still retain their remarkable power and freshness over the decades, it is surely because they are so rich, so multi-layered, so full of invention, ingenuity and insight. They provided the receptacle for so much creativity and so many ideas, lyrical and musical, and Pete and Clive have come back to it time and time again, filling the bucket to the brim. And because they put so much in, there is always more to be taken out.

When Clive says 'Writing song lyrics is my favourite form of writing anything', he's speaking with the voice of experience. He's tried everything, from *Peregrine Prykke's Pilgrimage Through the London Literary World*, an epic 50-page satirical ballad, written in 1974, to memoirs, criticism, serious essays on ethics, life and literature and the successful short verses that have solidified his reputation, over the last few years, as a poet of genuine worth and stature. But the songs still have a unique place in his heart. He treasures the knowledge that there are a few thousand people who have made these songs part of their lives, playing the albums, quoting the lyrics alongside the great lines from *Monty Python*, *Hitchhiker's Guide to the Galaxy* and *Blackadder* that infiltrated the speech of two whole generations, and often passing on their enthusiasm to their children.

'You can always hope for more,' he wrote, a few years ago, 'But those happy few should be enough to keep a songwriter going, if the song, and not the celebrity status, is what he really cares about.'

Celebrity status came to Clive via other routes. Cult status came, unsought, through the songs. The only surprise is the way the effects of Clive's fame failed to flow across the different media to bring the albums to a mass audience. But he and Pete have both done pretty well, anyway. And how many people have a sideline, apart from their mainstream careers, through which they can gain such fanatical appreciation and internal satisfaction?

The songwriting team that took its first tentative steps after hours in the Cambridge Footlights clubroom in the mid-Sixties has produced nearly 200 songs. When members of the online Midnight Voices fan club conducted a poll to find the best-loved Atkin/James creations, a few years ago, the vote was split across 58 different songs. A vigorous debate then followed, in which people who had failed to vote weighed in with nominations for another ten or twelve, outside the 58. When I called this book *Loose Canon*, it was partly this phenomenon that I had in the back of my head. The catalogue of songs is there, but it clearly looks very different for different people.

Fans who like the subtle musical and lyrical detailing that lifts the songs of love and loss out of the ordinary may have no time at all for what Pete and Clive call the 'history' songs – the ones that take us back to Ancient Troy, Israel in AD 33, the Vietnam War or the extermination of the Native Americans. Those who are drawn to the melodic clarity of the songs about music and musicians ('Thief in the Night', 'National Steel, 'Thirty Year Man' and 'Sessionman's Blues', among others) don't necessarily enjoy the abrasive urban edge of 'Rain-wheels' and 'I See the Joker' or the jagged words and music of 'The Wall of Death'. And while the songs can be grouped into loose categories like this for casual discussion, the individual tracks are so different that any attempt at categorisation soon seems pointless and unhelpful. Whether a particular composition happens to have started with the lyric or with the tune, the common characteristic of all Atkin/James songs is that they don't sound like each other, and they don't sound like anything else. That's made it hard to reach a mass audience, but it's given the non-mass audience many years of subtle and refined pleasures.

Clive talks about the day he met Pete as the day he 'found his musician'. As soon as they started collaborating, he knew he had discovered the soulmate who could help him fulfil his ambition to write clever, daring, original and beautifully crafted songs. For Pete, working with his partner's remarkable, unpredictable talent has been a privilege and a constant source of stimulation.

During his years in radio, Pete rubbed shoulders with many brilliant writers and wits, from Frank Muir and Denis Norden to Kenneth Williams, Martin Jarvis, Victoria Wood and Paul Merton. But he has no doubt about Clive's standing in this distinguished company.

'Clive is, by some considerable margin, the most talented person I have ever met at close quarters,' he told Radio 4 listeners in 2015, in a programme to celebrate the launch of the final album of Atkin/James songs, *The Colours of the Night*. 'He is a mighty, mighty figure. I just feel extraordinarily lucky to have hooked up with him.'

18

A Promising Career: Take 2

I once wrote a book about the internet (or the Internet, as we called it then). It was 1998 and the book was modestly titled *Mastering the Internet*. The publishers, Orion Business Books, were already committed to producing the book for their autumn list and they had carelessly lost the author who was supposed to be writing it for them, so I was roped in to do it at short notice. I had been at Orion's offices, delivering the manuscript for another book I'd co-written, called *NLP and the New Manager*, when the news came through that the internet expert had disappeared. This was causing some panic, as the manuscript needed to go to print in two months' time. I'd been reading a lot of books and articles about how this extraordinary new technology was going to change our world, and it seemed obvious to me that nobody really had the faintest idea about where it would lead us. So I volunteered to take it on, found a co-author who could fill me in on all the technical background and duly wrote the book to fit behind the title.

These days, *Mastering the Internet* reads like a historic document. The world it describes is almost unrecognisable and the bold claims I made for the future influence of the World Wide Web look ridiculously timid. I remember warning businesses not to underestimate the online market. Look, I said, there could be 30 or 40 million people out there, all round the world, who might want to buy your products. It's like having another big national market to target. It's like a Virtual Canada. You wouldn't want to ignore that many potential customers, would you?

Well, the world did change. Facebook alone has 1.5 billion users. My daring prediction that you might even order your groceries online for home delivery has come to pass. My tip for the top, a brand new search engine called Google, has gone on to add a new verb to the English language. And the internet has been responsible for all kinds of completely unexpected side-effects, including the resurrection of the songwriting partnership between Clive James and Pete Atkin.

By the mid-1990s, Clive and Pete were both doing well. But they weren't doing it together. Clive was jetting round the world, making offbeat, tongue-in-cheek television spectaculars. Pete had become a highly respected radio producer, working on much-loved programmes like *Just a Minute*, *Week Ending* and *This Sceptred Isle*, the BBC's 46-hour, 216-part history of Britain. The music had become a sideline and he was only playing a couple of gigs a year, 'just to keep my hand in'.

But one evening, at a folk club in Eastbourne, Pete was button-holed by a fan who had come, with his wife and son, on a 500-mile round trip from his home in Derbyshire to see him perform. The man was called Stephen Birkill. He was a real boffin, a top BBC transmission engineer and satellite television pioneer who had gone out on his own, designing efficient and ultra-cheap satellite receiver boxes for Alan Sugar's Amstrad in the 1980s and picking up a royalty of a few pence on every one of the millions of receivers the company produced. In later years, he went on to invent new types of tuner that were used in Freeview TV boxes and most of the digital radios sold in the UK and Europe.

Besides being a techie, Steve Birkill was also, by his own account, 'an obsessive', much given to quoting odd lines of Atkin/Jamesiana in ordinary conversation, to the bafflement of his friends. He'd seen Pete play a couple of times in the 1970s and had almost worn out his copies of the six Pete Atkin albums. Now he had come up with a plan to drag Pete out of his semi-retirement and lure him up to the Peak District.

'I wanted Pete to come and play in my backyard,' says Steve. 'I had a farmhouse and nine acres of pasture land near the village of Monyash and I wanted to set up a folk festival, with Pete at the centre of it, and try to get all the fans together in one place to hear him perform.'

When he mentioned this dream to Pete at the Eastbourne gig, along with the tentative suggestion that he might begin to put together a Pete Atkin web page, he was delighted with the positive response. Pete was all for it, and the planning went ahead, with Steve doing all he could, in those pre-Facebook, pre-Twitter, pre-everything days, to publicise the event online. In August 1997, 250 people turned up for the first Monyash Folk Festival, most of them apparently quite bemused to discover that there were others who shared their passion for these fondly-remembered songs of their youth. A huge marquee had been set up and Pete played a two-and-a-half-hour

31-song set, including several titles that had been demoed in the Seventies but never released on record, and surprised everyone by bringing on Julie Covington to sing four of the Atkin/James numbers from her first album.

Over the weekend of the festival, the idea came up again that the internet might offer a way for the fans who had turned up at Monyash, and others elsewhere in Britain and around the world, to stay in touch with each other, exchange news about gigs and spread the word that Pete was still alive and kicking. No-one was thinking of anything lavish at this stage, but a mailing list could be set up and Steve Birkill volunteered to put together an online discography and information page.

'It wasn't going to be much more than a simple Wikipedia-type page at first,' he says. 'But we soon found there were a lot more Atkin/James fans around than we'd thought – and enough of them were online to make it well worth doing.'

Within a few weeks, nine hundred people had joined the mailing list and the new online community, calling itself Midnight Voices, after a line from Clive's lyrics for 'Payday Evening', had become the focus for dozens of reminiscences of gigs past, guitar transcriptions of many of the songs, forensic analysis of the finer points of the lyrics and heated arguments about people's favourites.

Musicologists delved into the trademark touches that make Atkin songs so distinctive. 'But at one point in the middle eight there's a fabulous – and unforgettable – use of the tritone when the key jumps from G flat back to the dominant C for the line "You even weep for what did not take place",' remarked one admirer of 'The Magic

Wasn't There'. Guitarists weighed in with their admiration for Pete's 'idiosyncratic' and 'un-diatonic' chord sequences. Academics set off in pursuit of every quote, every reference and every veiled allusion to poets ancient and modern, while other self-appointed sleuths followed up all the mentions of historical, literary and Hollywood characters, rushing back to lay their findings at the feet of other Midnight Voices members like puppies proudly bringing frogs into the kitchen.

Over the next few months, the modest information page turned into a full-blown website. There were full lyrics for 150 Atkin/James songs and a music player that offered twenty of Pete's most popular tracks, alongside oddities like a recording of Kenny Everett hamming it up while introducing 'Master of the Revels' on Radio One.

Thanks to the internet, there was now ample evidence that an audience still existed for the Atkin/James catalogue. The people might be scattered far and wide, but the website provided a mechanism to bring them all together and create a forum for their enthusiasms and opinions.

As the Midnight Voices group gathered momentum, fans who had heard live performances of important but unrecorded songs like 'Canoe' and 'Search and Destroy' in the Seventies began urging Pete to produce another album. A renaissance was under way.

The next summer, Steve Birkill hired Buxton Opera House, ten miles down the road from Monyash, and put on another big concert. This time Clive came along, too, joining Pete for an evening of songs, poems and readings of scenes from his *Unreliable Memoirs*. It was the first time in twenty-three years that they had shared a stage, and, to everyone's surprise except Steve's, nearly 600 people turned up.

Clive sang with Pete on 'Laughing Boy' and gave a solo rendition of 'A Man Who's Been Around'. But the highlight of the evening was the first-ever performance, by Clive, of the stunning 'Hill of Little Shoes', about the children who died at Auschwitz. This was the first important new Atkin/James song for a quarter of a century, and Clive gave the fans full credit for inspiring the duo to pick up where they had left off in the Seventies.

'We are writing again, and we've got a lot of ideas that we want to explore, now we know that there are people who will listen,' he said. 'You Midnight Voices people have made it happen, because the website, with its chronicle of our songwriting history so far, has made me want to begin again.'

In 1999, there was another festival gig at Monyash. The fans warmed up in the afternoon with a Pete Atkin tribute band and Pete played a monster three-hour set in the evening. This performance marked another turning point, as it consisted largely of new or un-recorded songs and even omitted two of the big hits from his earlier incarnation, 'Beware of the Beautiful Stranger' and 'Girl on the Train'. The signals were clear. Though there was a vast bank of much-loved songs from the Seventies, Pete and Clive were not going to wallow in nostalgia. They were back in business, writing new material that was just as powerful, thought-provoking, enjoyable and unpredictable as the old favourites. Suddenly, Pete was being asked to perform in folk clubs and colleges around the country.

These days, Pete and Clive happily credit Steve Birkill as the man who restarted their songwriting career.

'Without Steve, our catalogue of recorded works would have

ended in the mid-Seventies,' says Pete. 'There are more than fifty songs that would never have seen the light of day, including some songs on *Winter Spring* and *The Colours of the Night* that are certainly among the best things we've ever done. The internet made it possible, but Steve made it happen. Knowing the Midnight Voices fans were out there guaranteed us a core audience – and that was what we needed to get the juices flowing again.'

The choice of Midnight Voices as the fan group's name was slightly odd, as the song the phrase comes from, 'Payday Evening', is a rather downbeat, wistfully sad number. When *The Road of Silk* came out in 1974, the *New Statesman* magazine's reviewer singled the track out for some pretty highbrow analysis.

'There is an elegiac air,' Charles Fox wrote, 'a stylish melancholy, surfacing most purely in "Payday Evening", lamenting the collapse of love as much as our 20th-century squalor, its despair somehow closer to Dowson or Arthur Symons or John Davidson than to the image of that wide-awake Aussie, that over-bright TV reviewer.'

I think that meant he liked it. The references to Ernest Dowson (the late-19th-century decadent poet who coined the phrase 'the days of wine and roses'), Arthur Symons (1865–1945) and John Davidson, the Scottish depressive who drowned himself in 1909, but whose poems strongly influenced Wallace Stevens and TS Eliot, must have been pretty obscure even then. Clive is not the only person who likes to show off his knowledge. But the man from the *New Statesman* was certainly taking the lyrics seriously. He couldn't resist the implicit dig at Clive for being popular in the mass media, but he did talk about him in poetic terms, as an 'unreconstructed Romantic, a Symbolist manqué', and he did urge him to put together a book about the art of writing lyrics. The reviewer was obviously right to pinpoint Clive's 'stylish melancholy', though, and 'Payday Evening' has that in abundance – both the melancholy and the style.

There's a lot in this lyric. It's a typical Clive trick to jolt the listener from the dingy gloom of a North London pub to the opulence of the gardens and theatres of Louis XV's court at Versailles and back again to the 'liquid circles on Formica tables'. There's a glancing reference to DH Lawrence's post-Great War poem 'Look! We Have Come Through!' in the line 'Somehow we have failed to come through' and a neatly ironic contrast between the apparent resignation of 'The poetic age has had its day' and the classically poetic eloquence of the last stanza:

> In midnight voices,
> Softer than a dove's,
> We shall talk superbly of our lost loves

But it is the scene outside the pub that sticks in the memory. The grim realism of the strung-out man trying to raise money by selling his girlfriend's body is emphasised by a pitiless close-up, zooming in on her haggard features.

> Outside a junkie tries to sell his girl.
> Her face has just begun to come apart.
> Look hard and you can see the edges curl.
> Speed has got her beaten at the start

The language is spare, largely monosyllabic, undecorative. The words sit squarely on the notes and the rhyme scheme has been tied down tight. In the first two verses, before the first of the bridge passages whisks us off to Versailles, only lines two and four rhyme. By now, though, there is a strict ABAB rhyming pattern, imposing an extra discipline and marking the line endings more sharply. The unaccompanied piano behind the early verses has gradually been augmented by bass, drums and, finally, taut and held-back electric guitar, and the song builds towards the muted crescendo of a thoughtful guitar solo, the length of a full 30-second verse, before tapering down to the gently lyrical ending.

Payday Evening

WORDS BY CLIVE JAMES, MUSIC BY PETE ATKIN

Of late I try to kill my payday evenings
In many an unrecommended spot,
Curiosity accounting for a little,
Loneliness accounting for a lot

The girls who pull the handles force their laughter.
The casual conversation's not the best,
Indifference accounting for a little,
Unhappiness accounting for the rest

And the gardens of the heyday in Versailles
And Pompadour's theatre in the stairs
Should be created in my magic eye
From a jukebox and a stack of canvas chairs

But somehow we have failed to come through.
The styles are gone to seed, no more parades.
There seems to be no talk of me and you,
No breath of scandal in these sad arcades

Concerning us there are no fables,
No brilliant poems airily discarded.
Just liquid circles on Formica tables,
A silence perhaps too closely guarded

Outside a junkie tries to sell his girl.
Her face has just begun to come apart.
Look hard and you can see the edges curl.
Speed has got her beaten at the start

And what care these two for a broken heart?

The lady's calling 'Time' and she is right.
My time has come to find a better way,
A surer way to navigate at night.
The poetic age has had its day

In midnight voices,

Softer than a dove's,

We shall talk superbly of our lost loves.

We shall talk superbly of our lost loves

19

Lunar Perspectives

In 1969, two American astronauts, Neil Armstrong and Buzz Aldrin, landed on the moon. Yes, they did. Despite all the easily-deflated conspiracy theories that have entertained millions over the years, Armstrong's small step for a man was indeed 'a giant leap for mankind'. It may not have led on anywhere much over the last half-century, but it most certainly happened.

If nothing else, the fact that the other world superpower, the Communist bloc, would have given anything – thousands of lives, billions of roubles, whatever it took – to undermine America's achievement, and failed to do so, proves the point beyond doubt. Another five Apollo missions and ten more sets of footprints followed, and we got used to the idea that there would soon be permanent manned bases on the moon. Not immediately, we understood that. But within twenty years, maybe, or thirty. After all, the first moon landing had taken place just six years after President John F Kennedy had announced the ambition to go there. Now that the breakthrough had been made, the solar system was our oyster.

Back home on Planet Earth, Clive and Pete, like all the song-writers of the previous sixty years, were busy writing songs about the moon. But they weren't, at that time, writing explicitly about the Apollo missions. When they composed 'Be Careful When They Offer You the Moon', it was much more in the time-honoured moon-rhymes-with-June tradition – though they wouldn't have been heard dead using that particular rhyme. The song they wrote starts by taking a fairly conventional view of the moon, talking about its cold light ('only ever made to light the night'), saying it's 'built for dead souls' and dismissing it as 'a colourless and dusty ball of holes'. Gently, though, the more topical references begin to creep in. 'You can break an ankle dancing on the moon' is not the sort of comment Fred Astaire or anyone else would have made before the idea of stepping out into low gravity became a reality. And the middle eight effectively puts you up there yourself, looking down on the home planet and its petty disappointments.

When you take the moon you kiss the world goodbye
For a chance to lord it over loneliness.
And a quarter-million miles down the sky
They'll watch you shining more but weighing less

We're still focused on the moon itself in the last verse, distracted by the Paper Moon theme and lulled by the cheery elegance of Clive's words. 'It's only dream stuff,' he warns. 'It's a Tin Pan Alley prop held up by bluff / And nobody breathes easy on the moon.'

But you should never turn your back on a wordslinger. All through the song, the lyric has been advising us to exercise caution when they offer us the moon. And have we listened? Have we hell. As we turn into the last line, we've been set up for a classic sucker punch. 'Count to ten when they offer you the moon' changes the whole impact of the song. This isn't about looking up at the heavens. It's about keeping your feet on the ground and counting your fingers after shaking hands with the sort of people who promise you the earth.

'Be Careful When They Offer You the Moon' was originally recorded for release as a single, several months after the sessions for the first album, *Beware of the Beautiful Stranger*. When it came out, backed by 'Master of the Revels', the track that Kenny Everett played to death on his Sunday morning Radio One show, there was some confusion among the DJs about which of these two very different songs was meant to be the A-side and the record eventually sank from view. When RCA reissued *Beware of the Beautiful Stranger* three years later, 'Touch Has a Memory' was dropped from the album and 'Be Careful When They Offer You the Moon' was brought in to replace it.

Much later in their career, though, during the long gap of twenty-five years between *Live Libel* and the privately-distributed *Lakeside Sessions* double album, Clive and Pete looped back on themselves to polish and revive a set of lyrics Clive had begun writing in 1970. This was another, very different, song about the moon. This time it was a dramatic retelling of the story of Apollo 13, the moonshot mission that went badly wrong and nearly made martyrs of its three-man crew.

Apollo 13's problems started two days into the flight when an oxygen tank exploded, 200,000 miles above the earth. Short of power, water and oxygen, the three men on board had to wait more than three days, while the spaceship swung round the far side of the moon and limped back towards earth, before facing up to the life-or-death drama of re-entry. The world watched, glued to the TV screen, as the astronauts grappled with the challenge of getting home safely and millions sighed with relief when the parachutes finally opened and the battered spacecraft floated down into the South Pacific.

Clive's lyrics for this song, 'Canoe', are among his most unusual. There is no rhyme scheme at all and the shape of the song is dictated by its subtle rhythms, based on the use of Shakespearean iambic pentameters in the first two lines and last line of each verse. But it isn't its unconventional form that makes 'Canoe' stand out. It's the extraordinary idea of drawing a dramatic parallel between three South Sea islanders making a perilous and ultimately fatal voyage in their canoe and the three astronauts whose lives hung by a thread as Apollo 13 struggled to get back to earth.

There is no introduction of the metaphor, no line that says 'It's like drifting in a canoe, trying to hit a tiny target point in an ocean of threats and danger.' The song starts with the three Polynesians, proud of having been chosen for their mission, setting out to steer by the stars and find the distant island where they can carry out their mission of bartering their people's shells for feathers. As the days go by and the sun beats down, they realise that their navigation hasn't been good enough. They've missed the island. They are lost, adrift in the vastness of the Pacific, and their fate is sealed.

What happens next is extraordinary. The two lines that follow form a hinge point, facing both backwards and forwards and wrenching the song in a totally new direction. 'The time had come for all of us to die / "She's out a whole degree" takes us straight from the canoe into the spacecraft, where any tiny deviation in the angle of descent threatens to spell the end for the three American astronauts. The computers are switched off and the men find themselves having to fly the ship manually, using their own skill and judgement to enter the atmosphere at just the right angle to avoid disintegrating in a shower of sparks. Like the three canoeists, they have only their own talents to rely on. But unlike the doomed Polynesians, they get away with it and 'the lucky three' are able to return safely to their families.

On first hearing, this abrupt shift could be potentially confusing. But it doesn't seem to work that way. Pete's music – a strange, insistent, piano-led tune – holds the song together, both in solo performances and on the *Lakeside Sessions* album (more formally known as *History and Geography: The Lakeside Sessions, Vol 1*), which finally saw the light of day in 2001. On the album, the piano is supported by subtly atmospheric drums and a tactfully understated bass part, but it is the interplay between the voice and piano that defines the song's pace and atmosphere and makes it all work.

Clive was astonished and delighted to see how his co-writer had managed to fuse the two parts of the song into a coherent whole.

'Pete joined the two stories together so subtly that even I couldn't see the join,' he said, years later. 'Looking back on it now, I feel that this was one of the important transitional songs for us, pointing forward to the kind of songs we would write much later, in the second part of our career.'

That second coming of Clive James and Pete Atkin represented a remarkable renewal of the creative partnership. Besides the 28 songs recorded on the two *Lakeside Sessions* CDs (the other is *A Dream of Fair Women: The Lakeside Sessions, Vol 2)*, it led to another two albums made up mostly of new compositions. *Winter Spring*, released in 2003, contains two of the finest Atkin/James songs, 'Dancing Master' and 'A Hill of Little Shoes' (and Clive's own personal favourite from their entire catalogue, 'Winter Spring' itself), while the last album, *The Colours of the Night*, has some lovely tunes and a new warmth and apparent simplicity of the sort that tends to come with forty-plus years of practice and experience.

'Canoe' quickly became a favourite with the dedicated Pete Atkin fans. But it also managed to get through to people who had no idea what to expect. When Pete and Clive played their fourteen-date 'Words and Music' tour together in Australia, in 2003, it was received with great enthusiasm. With no rhymes, no clever-clogs wordplay and the apparent disadvantage of its strange two-part structure, it was an unlikely hit. Yet there is something powerful and almost eerie about the way the words and music sit together, and audiences pick up on this. By the time we reach the end, even the gentle rhythm of the lines 'The parachutes deployed / We were rocking like a cradle / As we drifted down in silence to the sea' seems to be doing its bit, unwinding the tension and drawing the song to a safe and serene conclusion.

Clive has spoken many times about his conviction that popular songs should be able to talk about anything, to handle any kind of subject. On the surface, 'Canoe' is about a space mission. At another level, though, it touches on deeper themes. It's about the human ambition to challenge the unknown. It's about how we, as people, relate to the universe around us, and why and how different societies are prepared to send their young men out on fruitless and dangerous missions. And it's about how these themes persist through every generation and culture.

The technology and the geography change, but the story doesn't. There is always a canoe and an ocean of perilous and uncharted waters to sail it on. And there is always the moon, 'waning through the nights and days', drawing men's eyes upwards and outwards, hypnotising lovers and confusing navigators, inspiring con-men and luring astronauts to risk their lives. 'Be careful,' as the song says, 'when they offer you the moon.' You never quite know what you might be getting yourself into.

Canoe

WORDS BY CLIVE JAMES, MUSIC BY PETE ATKIN

The perfect moon was huge above the sea.
The surf was easy, even on the reef.
We were the lucky three
Who slid in our canoe
Through the flowers on the water
And tried to read the signals in the sky

We travelled with our necklaces of shell.
The moon was waning through the nights and days.
And how we dreamed of home.

But we couldn't find the island
Where you trade the shells for feathers.
We fainted in the sun's reflected blaze

With cracking lips, I turned to tell my friends
The time had come for all of us to die.
'She's out a whole degree,'
I told them as I floated,
Checking readouts at my shoulder.
'Re-enter at this angle and we'll fry'

The go for override came up from earth.
We took control and we flew her with our hands.
And how we dreamed of home.
We saw the South Pacific
As we fought to get her zeroed
Before the heatshield started hitting air

We came home in a roaring purple flame
And gave the mission back to the machines.
We were the lucky three.
The parachutes deployed.
We were rocking like a cradle,
As we drifted down in silence to the sea

20

Changing Places

You know how it works. Clive James writes the words. Pete Atkin writes the music and does the singing. That's how it is. Mostly. But there are a handful of songs where the usual division of labour breaks down. In the early part of this book, I admitted that I had been fooled by the one track on the first album that was entirely written by Pete, convincing myself that I could see in its neat form, wording and structure the supposedly unmistakeable fingerprints of Clive's style. And today, attached to an email from Pete, I found a recording I had never heard before, featuring Julie Covington singing the only song Clive ever wrote the music for, as well as the words.

This brisk 1930s showtune-style number is called 'The Paper Wing Song'. It was written back in 1967, when Pete and Clive were putting together the songs for their very first, hand-knitted, 160-copy limited edition album, *While the Music Lasts*.

The first thing to say about it is that it's not bad at all. In fact, it's a very attractive song. Leaving aside the fact that Julie could sing the telephone directory (if such things still existed) and make it sound good, Clive managed to come up with a fast, catchy little tune that neatly complements his words. His bare melody was fleshed out by

Pete and Clive's Cambridge Footlights friend Daryl Runswick, who was already playing bass with Johnny Dankworth and went on to become a successful composer and to play with or for an unusually wide range of collaborators, from Elton John and Ornette Coleman to Pierre Boulez and Simon Rattle.

'I think Clive thought humming a melody line was all you had to do to be a composer,' says Pete, sounding suspiciously like an old-time trade union leader protecting his turf and laying down the law in a demarcation dispute. 'Daryl did the rest, adding the chords and harmonies and helping him turn it from an idea into a song.'

'The Paper Wing Song' is an early example of Clive's surprisingly shaky grasp of how popular song titles work. Why not just 'Paper Wings', a phrase that occurs three times at key points in the song? He has often opted for label titles like this, most disastrously in relation to 'An Array of Passionate Lovers', an interesting song on *The Road of Silk* about the end of the Flower Power Love Generation, which would surely have caught the imagination more readily if it had picked up on one of the lines in the lyric. If the title had been 'Children of the Dream' or the opening line, 'The Troops of Love Are Pulling Out', the words would have helped remind people of the tune and this reinforcement would have made the song vastly more memorable.

But there's plenty to like about 'The Paper Wing Song', both in the words and the music. The first verse sets the scene and introduces the key phrase.

The Magic Wasn't There

With just a word, a single sign of care
With just a touch, I could have been beguiled
But circumstances never smiled
Because the magic wasn't there.

Who was it then, the poet who once said
How beautiful they are, the trains you miss?
So time can't put an end to this;
I have the memory instead.

These nothing scenes are still experience
You even weep for what did not take place
Events that don't occur are still events.
Some people vanish with a trace.

With just a word, a single sign of care
With just a touch, I could have been beguiled
But circumstances never smiled
And now what never happened drives me wild
Because the magic wasn't there.

~ Clive James
Cambridge Nov 26, 88
for music by
Pete Atkin.

No hit, but a near miss: Julie Covington's soulful cover version of 'The Magic Wasn't There' spent four weeks just outside the Top 40.

Have you Got a Biro I Can Borrow

Have you got a biro I can borrow?
I'd like to write your name
On the palm of my hand, the walls of the hall
The roof of the house, right across the land:
So when the sun comes up tomorrow
It'll look to this side of the hard-bitten planet
Like a big yellow button with your name written on it.

Have you got a biro I can borrow?
I'd like to write some lines
In praise of your knee and the back of your neck
And the double decker bus that brings you to me:
So when the sun comes up tomorrow
It'll shine on a world made richer by a sonnet
And [a] half a dozen epics as long as the Aeneid.

~~Oh give me a pen, give me some paper~~
Oh give me a pen and some paper
Give me a chisel or a camera,
A piano and a box of rubber bands:
~~Give me~~ I need room for choreography
And a dark room for photography —
Tie the brush into my hands!

[From last light to first]

Have you got a biro I can borrow?
I'd like to write your name
From the belt of Orion to the share of the Plough
And the snout of the Bear to the belly of the Lion :
So when the sun goes down tomorrow,
[From start to finish] there'll never be a minute,
Not a moment, of the night that hasn't got you in it.

↓

— Clive James
Cambridge
Dec 8th 1967.

Have you got a biro I can borrow?
I'd like to write your name
From the belt of Orion to the share of the Plough
And the snout of the Bear to the belly of the Lion :
So when the sun goes down tomorrow,
[From last light to first] there'll never be a minute,
Not a moment, of the night that hasn't got you in it.

Got it! The key to the elegant change of pace in the last verse of this enduringly popular Atkin/James favourite was the removal of 'From last light to first'.

Touch Has A Memory
(gloss on a line by Keats)

Touch has a memory
   Better than the other senses'
Hearing and sight ~~fight~~ free (win)
Touching has no defences

Textures come back to you, real as can be
Touch has a memory.

Fine eyes are wide at night
Eyelashes show that nicely
Seeing forgets the sight
Touch recollects precisely

Eyelids are modest yet blink at a kiss
Touching takes note of this.

When, in a later day
Little of the vision lingers
Memory slips away
Every way but through the fingers

Textures come back to you, real as can be
Making you feel
Time doesn't heal
And touch has a memory.

Clive James
Cambridge 1967
for music by Pete Atkin.

Waxing poetic: This delicate song was based on a phrase filched from John Keats. Note the calligraphic flourishes, quite unlike Clive's usual handwriting.

History and Geography

The history and geography of feeling less than wonderful is known to me
The dates of broken bubbles and the whereabouts of every lost belief
And from the Point of Tears I see how far away across the Sea of Troubles
The Pinnacles of Happiness are halfway hidden in the Clouds of Grief.

My common sense can tell me all it likes to count myself among the lucky
For pity's sake to draw a breath and take a look around me and compare
My growing-pains against the sack and rack and ruin of an open city
On a village caught between the anvil of the ground and hammer of the air.
But when I breathe again the
the Thought Peace of Satisfaction and the way
But still the little happiness and how it slips away from you defeats you   me
The flowing speech that stuttered out, the pretty song that faded on the
page/air
And the man who raids a garbage can and coughs his stale crumbs into the
gutter
At least may count himself among the choice and master spirits of the age.

Without a home, without a name, a girl of whom to say this is my sister
For I am all the daughters of my father's house and all the brothers too
I comb the rubble of a shattered world to find the bright face of an angel
And say again and say again that I have written this, this is for you.
broken

When the jet returns me half awake and half asleep to what I call my
homeland
I look down into the midnight city through the empty inkwell of the sky
And in that kit of instruments laid out across a velvet-covered table
I know that nothing lives which doesn't hold its place more worthily than I.

The history and geography of feeling less than wonderful is known to me
When sunsets are unlovely and the dawns are coldly calculated light
And from the Heights of Arrogance across the Steps that Later I Regretted
I see those angel faces flame their last and flicker out into the night.

I see those angel faces flame their last and flicker out into the night.

                              Clive James
                              for music by
                              Pete Atkin
                              Cambridge
                              April 1969

But what: the sense of common sense when feeling less than wonderful defeats me?

But am I sure to see and hear to something I'm unable to remember

History rewritten: The smoothly-crafted words that found their way into Pete's
2001 *Lakeside Sessions* recording gave no hint of the reshaping that had gone on.

THE HYPERTENSION KID

Last night I met the Hypertension Kid *Grimly chasing shorts with*
~~Chasing scotches with a half of bitter~~ / *shots with halves* *halves of bitter*
In a Mayfair club they call the Early Quitter
He met my eyes and hit me for a quid

"I spend fortunes in this rat-trap" said the Kid
"But the plush and flock soak up the brain's kerfuffle
And I like to see a servile barman shuffle
If sympathy's your need, let's hear your bid"

"It's my lousy memory" I told the Kid
"What other men forget I still remember
The flies are still alive inside the amber
It's a garbage can with rubbish for a lid"

"Your metaphors are murder" said the Kid
"I know the mood - give into it a little
The man who shatters is the man who's ~~brittle~~ *brittle*
Lay off the brakes and steer into the skid"

"Strained virtue warps the soul" announced the Kid
"Those forced attempts at cleanliness that linger
Like soap between your wedding ring and finger
They're residues of which you're better rid"

"For evil" said the Hypertension Kid
"Is better contemplated in the deeds of others
Mass-murderers and men who knife their mothers
Be glad that what you've done is <u>all</u> you did"

"With me the problem's women" said the Kid
"Befuddled, fondled, under separate covers
And one and all they've gone to other lovers
As I powered down to zero from the grid

"But I love the little darlings" sighed the Kid
"The slide from grace is really more like gliding
And I've found the trick is not to stop the sliding
But to find a graceful way of staying slid

"As for the dreadful memories" said the Kid
"The wasteland poison in the spirit's river
Relax your hands and let the bastards quiver
They tremble more, the more you keep it hid"

We turned to leave the bar, me and the Kid
I with (a) lightened head and lessened terror
Towards the street, and he into the mirror:
~~My life-long guide and running mate in error~~
My *second* self, the Hypertension Kid

Clive James
music - Pete Atkin

Second thoughts: The line 'My life-long guide and running mate in error' would
have blunted the final twist. Happily, it never saw the light of day.

BE CAREFUL WHEN THEY OFFER YOU THE MOON

Be careful when they offer you the moon.
It gives a cold light.
It was only ever made to light the night.
You can freeze your fingers handling the moon.

Be careful when they offer you the moon,
It's built for dead souls.
It's a colourless and dusty ball of ~~holes~~ holes.
You can break an ankle dancing on the moon.

(BR) When you take the moon you kiss the world goodbye
For a chance to lord it over loneliness
And a quarter million miles down the sky
They'll watch you shining more but weighing less.

So be careful when they offer you the moon
It's only dream stuff.
It's a Tin Pan Alley prop held up by bluff
And nobody breathes easy on the moon.

Count to ten when they offer you the moon.

Clive James
for music by Pete Atkin
London Cambridge
November 17th, 1989.

Right first time: No alterations, and Clive's even marked the stresses on 'cold',
'dead' and 'dream'. The last line, of course, turns the whole song on its head.

```
PAYDAY EVENING

Of late I try to kill my payday evenings
In many an unrecommended spot
Curiosity accounting for a little
And loneliness accounting for a lot

The girls who pull the handles force their laughter
And the casual conversation's not the best
Indifference accounting for a little
Unhappiness accounting for the rest

And the gardens of the heyday in Versailles
And Pompadour's theatre in the stairs
Should be recreated in my magic eye
From a jukebox and a stack of canvas chairs

But somehow we have failed to come through
The styles are gone to seed - no more parades
There seems to be no talk of me and you
No breath of scandal in these sad arcades

Concerning us there are no fables
No Or brilliant poems airily discarded
Just liquid circles on formica tables
A silence perhaps too closely guarded

And no-one in this place knows who I am
They fail to recognise the last flaneur
The cynosure of Kurfurstendamm
So how could they imagine what you were?
What's Hecuba to them, or them to her?

The lady's calling time and she is right
My time has come to find a better way
A surer way to navigate at night
The poetic age has had its day

Outside a hippie tries to sell his girl
Whose face has just begun to come apart
Look hard and you can see the edges curl
A has got her beaten at the start
And what care these two for a broken heart?

So come, Romantics, join me in the dark
At home the key is underneath the mat
They are beating someone senseless in the park
But behind a peeling door my basement flat
Has room enough to swing a stunted cat

In midnight voices softer than a dove's
We shall talk superbly of our lost loves

                    Clive James
```

'The last flâneur / The cynosure of Kurfürstendamm', forsooth! 'Payday Evening' sailed close to the wind, but was rescued by the deletion of two overripe verses.

I had a phase
Of doing silly things.
I did these crazy
Willy-nilly things.
To be with you
I'd put on paper wings

Within a couple of stanzas, the Jamesian word-juggling is in full flow. The girl's 'half-laughing love' is just the sort of thing young people fall for: 'Pups call it calf- / Calves call it puppy-love.' The ghost of Cole Porter is clearly hovering over Clive's pen as he warms to his task, basking in his ability to pull off party tricks involving complicated, multi-line sentence structures and demanding techniques like enjambement.

Dignity flew.
I didn't give a damn
Whether they knew
I'd come to live a sham-
-bles of a life,
Simply to be with you.

It's exhibitionist stuff, of course. But flipping the meaning across a broken word at the end of the line, so that 'I'd come to live a sham' turns into 'I'd come to live a shambles of a life' is ingenious, and curiously satisfying for the listener. The words dance nimbly across the light, jazzy rhythm and the song works, even in the original, hissy recording from almost half a century ago. Even now, it's the sort of hidden treasure someone like Diana Krall might stumble across and have some fun with.

After 'The Paper Wing Song', Clive left the music to Pete, though they would talk a lot about sounds and ideas as a song was coming into focus. If Pete came up with a tune Clive didn't think was suitable for a particular song, he'd have another go at it, carefully squirrelling the first tune away in his notebooks, to be trotted out, sometimes years later, when another set of lyrics seemed to fit it. Little was binned or wasted and many a discarded idea returned to the fray eventually, speeded up or slowed down, set to a different chord progression or with a longer or shorter line length. On the last album, *The Colours of the Night*, there are even two songs ('The Colours of the Night' and 'Last Ditch') with exactly the same lyric, though it seems to mean quite different things in the different versions. Clive wanted the more martial, upbeat tune ('Last Ditch'); Pete liked the desolate, fatalistic atmosphere of the other version. So they did both.

The collaborative process worked in both directions. Clive quickly discovered that Pete could find ways to accommodate the most amorphous and eccentric verse forms, if he had to. But sometimes accommodating an awkwardly shaped lyric was not the best thing for the song. Pete would suggest a change, a repeat or an extra line and they'd work out, between them, how they could make the music and the words sit well together.

And, once in a blue moon, Pete's own long-suppressed lyric-writing talents would come to the surface. Apart from 'All I Ever

Did' and 'The Original Original Honky Tonk Night Train Blues', both on *Beware of the Beautiful Stranger*, there were no Atkin/Atkin songs on any of the commercial albums until the very last, *Live Libel*. This record – 'the contractual fulfilment album' – was largely made up of topical parodies of music business giants, but it also included Pete's early song, 'Ballad of an Upstairs Window', written before he'd even met Clive. It had been his Footlights audition piece and it served him well over the years as light relief in folk club gigs, but this comic shaggy dog story had none of the well-turned elegance of 'All I Ever Did'. The style is almost music hall and the tale of a gormless hero who stands outside his girlfriend's house, looking up at her window, and refuses to recognise the significance of the motorbike parked outside her gate is only faintly hilarious.

> I felt compelled to cogitate
> On what was most appropriate
> In circumstances previously unknown.
> I reasoned that if she felt tired
> She wouldn't thank me if I woke her up
> And so I caught the bus back home

But Pete has a lot more to offer than this, as he showed when he wrote 'Over the High Side', one of the songs that would have been on the seventh commercial album, if the contract with RCA had been renewed or another record deal had been secured.

This is a sad, wistful song about losing the friends of our youth.

'Over the high side' is a motorcycling term for how not to part company with your bike in a crash. Low side falls are usually relatively safe; going over the high side, flying upwards and forwards off the bike, spells trouble and can often be fatal. The song describes the two friends as teenagers, 'Doing our best to look surly, / Killing time by kicking walls and talking loud', getting Saturday jobs to earn the down payments for the things they dream of. The narrator wants a guitar, but his friend wants a motorbike. Later, much later, when the narrator tries to track down his long-lost buddy and no-one at his number recognises the name, the realisation dawns that bikes are much more dangerous as hobbies than guitars and that the friend may already be dead.

'Over the High Side' is simple and direct, with a soulful chorus, a thoughtful, tender melody and a slow, even pace that leaves plenty of room for Pete's gracefully moody piano part. Unlike 'All I Ever Did', it doesn't sound at all like a Clive James composition. But it is a reminder that there are many ways to write successful songs and that Pete, like his long-time partner, has a remarkable ability to find the right words to tell a carefully-nuanced story.

Over the High Side

WORDS AND MUSIC BY PETE ATKIN

Summer nights we'd hang around our usual crowd,
Doing our level best to look surly.
Killing time by kicking walls and talking loud.
Wishing to hell our hair wasn't curly.

We laughed at the same old stories time and again.
Together so much we believed we'd be always friends

What can I say to you now?
What can I say to you now?
It's been a long, long time.
Too long

What can I say to you now?
What can I say to you now?
It's been a long, long time.
Too long

We both got weekend jobs to raise the money down,
Me for my first guitar, you for your bike.
But in the end I never even knew that you'd left town.
I tried to call you once, but – you know what it's like.
No-one at your number knew your name.
For all I knew, you'd gone over the high side in the rain

What can I say to you now?
What can I say to you now?
It's been a long, long time.
Too long

What can I say to you now?
What can I say to you now?

It's been a long, long time.

Too long

Too long

Too long

21

Dancing Mastery

In the early 1960s, I sat, in my black blazer and grey shorts, at an iron-framed desk in a classroom that hadn't changed since the 1890s, sweating over my Latin verbs. I can't remember much about it, except that the cover of every boy's copy of the textbook had been carefully defaced, over the generations, so that 'The Approach to Latin' became 'The Approach to Eating'. We had to make our own entertainment in those days.

When we got as far as third conjugation verbs, I was delighted to come across 'tango, tangere, tetigi, tactum – to touch'. 'Tango,' I thought. 'I can remember that. That's a dance.'

As usual, I was wrong. 'Tango' does mean 'to touch' in Latin, even now. But the derivation of our word for the dance, which originated in Argentina and Uruguay in the late nineteenth century, is actually thought to be from a term introduced by slaves from the Congo and meaning 'a closed place where people go to dance'.

Apart from vague childhood memories of Louis Armstrong's 'Two to Tango' and Alma Cogan's ghastly 'Never Do a Tango with an Eskimo', I had no idea what tango was about. The dictionary said it was a ballroom dance 'characterised by marked rhythms and postures, long, gliding steps and sudden pauses'. It didn't say it was an art form.

In fact, of course, tango is about love and lust, grace and beauty, movement and stillness, joy and sorrow, skill and spirit, tension and control. And so, you might say, is life.

Tango has fascinated Clive for years, and he has taken it seriously. He had a dance-floor installed upstairs in his flat in the Barbican, so he could practise regularly. He danced in London, he danced in Sydney whenever he went home and he flew to Buenos Aires, once or twice a year, for tango lessons with the masters. And eventually he wrote a great, poignant song about tango and about a master of the craft and his relationship with a very special student.

She's younger than him, of course. But she is a woman, rather than a girl. In this anxious, post-Savile era, it is only too easy to detect a whiff of paedophilia where nothing of the sort exists. In Britain, dancing lessons are almost exclusively about the young, about young girls pursuing the weekly round of ballet, tap and modern. We don't generally feel the need for adult dancing tuition – perhaps because we are so well endowed, as a nation, with our natural British gifts of rhythm and movement.

Tango is different, though. Tango is not a dance form for the young. Stylised and disciplined though it is, it is always, invariably, about sex. If all dancing is a perpendicular expression of a horizontal desire, as George Bernard Shaw so memorably claimed, tango is that in spades. After seeing the great Argentinian Osvaldo Zotto dance in London, Clive wrote that he seriously thought of 'tearing up every poem I had ever written and making arrangements to be born again in Buenos Aires'.

The fact that he had been born in the wrong place and come to the dance relatively late didn't stop him becoming an ardent and determined student. Just as he'd taught himself Italian, first, then Russian and even some Japanese so that he could understand and appreciate the literature and cultures better, he threw himself into learning tango. 'This is a language in which fluency costs a lifetime,' he said. From the 1990s onwards, the study of its grammar and vocabulary became a passion of his.

Clive dances no more. But his knowledge of tango informed one of his finest 21st-century songs.

Alongside 'An Empty Table', 'Winter Spring' and 'A Hill of Little Shoes', inspired by photos of the mound of children's footwear discovered by the liberators of Auschwitz, 'Dancing Master' is one of four standout tracks on 2003's *Winter Spring*, the first Pete Atkin album of newly-written songs since the mid-1970s.

During the long break from lyric writing, Clive had changed. When he and Pete started composing again, his style was generally leaner and more understated. In 'Dancing Master', the lyrics are simple, unshowy, naturalistic. There's not a word of more than two syllables, and there's none of the exuberant wordplay and outrageously inventive imagery of so many Atkin/James classics. The portrait of the tango teacher, racked by a wild desire that must be channelled through the discipline of his art, is painted with delicate, subtle brushstrokes and muted touches of colour.

'This is the step we'll learn tonight,' the dancing master tells his pupil. 'Turn on a dime and stay upright. Come back slowly, in your own time. I'll wait for you.' The wording is completely natural and conversational. The rhymes seem simple, the pairing of similar-sounding words ('learn' and 'turn', 'dime' and 'time', 'stay' and 'wait') so unforced that it could almost be accidental. Yet the rhythm beats through every line like the pulse of a muffled drum, the words and music as intimately intertwined as the hooked-together legs of the dancers performing tango's *gancho* movement.

The teacher, of course, is thinking of more than just the dance. 'This is the way the step looks best,' he says out loud. 'Keep it neat, as you come to rest.' Inside, he is completing the sentence with words that must remain unspoken: 'And if my heart seems to skip a beat, just wait for me.'

The dancing master is not going to spoil it all by stepping out of line or making a wrong move. He's grateful for what he has ('I have enough to last me') and he's resigned to getting nothing more ('What a man's never had he will never miss'). The silent worship of the woman is an end in itself. As he moves towards his own end, the ageing tango master's one wish is for these lessons to continue, for his courtly, unrequited love to carry on giving shape and meaning to his week.

The essence of tango is control and precision. It is a creative art form (honoured, since 2009, on UNESCO's Intangible Cultural Heritage list). But it is an art form that depends on taming the wild fires of passion, sublimating the urges of mind and body and transmuting these elements, by a subtle alchemy, into a pure and exquisite essence of style and poise. In this vivid song of desire, frustration and acceptance, Clive's lyrics neatly echo the formal disciplines of tango to create a perfect miniature.

Pete's contribution, as usual, lifts and supports the words without ever getting in the way. 'Dancing Master' is one of his finest vocal performances on record and the simple, restrained tune – the rhythm is technically a beguine, rather than a tango – is ideal for the task, backed up by a husky, close-miked alto sax solo from Patrick Reinhardt that hints at the vast unexplored hinterland of emotion that's kept in check by the dancing master's dedication to his art and his love.

This song is one of Clive and Pete's least-known gems. The *Lakeside Sessions* albums had slipped out almost unnoticed, except by the die-hard fans. *Winter Spring* effectively came out of the blue, more than a quarter of a century after the last commercially-produced album, and the sales were predictably modest. But it was worth waiting for. Even among dyed-in-the-wool Atkin/James enthusiasts, there are many who have never heard it. I can only envy them the pleasure that lies in wait for them when they meet the dancing master for the first time.

Dancing Master

WORDS BY CLIVE JAMES, MUSIC BY PETE ATKIN

As the world goes past me,
I have enough to last me,
As long as you come to call
And hang your coat and hat on the hook in the hall

This is the step we'll learn tonight.
Turn on a dime and stay upright.
Come back slowly, in your own time.
I'll wait for you

And as the world goes past me,
I have enough to last me,
As long as we dance like this.
What a man's never had, he will never miss

This is the way the step looks best.
Keep it neat, as you come to rest.
And if my heart seems to skip a beat,
Just wait for me

Just wait for me the way I wait for you,
For all the endless hours in a week.
This is the silent language lovers speak
When they mean nothing except what's true

Just wait for me the way I wait for you
To change your shoes before we say goodbye.
This the world where I will never die
Or lie awake for what I'm going through

And as the world goes past me,
I have enough to last me,

As long as we dance like that.

There's a hook in the hall

And it's waiting for your coat and hat

22

A Hill of Little Shoes

In January 1945, when Soviet troops entered the gates of Auschwitz, Clive James was five years old. The knowledge of the unbelievable horror of the biggest mass murder in history was something he grew up with over the years that followed, a terrible fact of 20th-century life that illuminated the best and worst in humanity, and he wrote about it time and time again in his most weighty prose essays. For him it was a matter 'too sacred to admit any experimentation', but that didn't mean it should be ruled out as the subject for poetry, or even song.

For all the flip wisecracks, romantic curlicues and satirical barbs of so many Atkin/James compositions, Clive and Pete have always stoutly maintained that nothing should be out of bounds to the ambitious songwriter. And in the late Nineties, prompted by the memory of the stark, black-and-white photographs that recorded the scenes inside the death camp, Clive wrote the lyrics for his most unflinchingly serious song, 'A Hill of Little Shoes'.

Auschwitz itself is never named. It doesn't need to be. The image of a huge pile of children's shoes is all too familiar, and it belongs to just one awful time and place in our past. But Clive's poetry and lyrics, at their best, are always, in some way, about him, and a large element in the success of this song is the way he relates directly to the tragedy he's writing about. Those children were his exact contemporaries. 'They were like you in the same year,' the song says. 'But you grew up / They were scarcely even here / Before they suddenly weren't there.'

The points of reference that bring the tragedy close to home are familiar to everyone who has ever had children. They are the domestic details parents know – the marks on the doorframe that measure a child's growth, the fierce concentration that goes into doing up buckles and laces and the earnest effort to 'be tall'. They're handled deftly, staying just the right side of sentimentality. There's no sign here of flashy wordplay or literary name-dropping and the only metaphor that's used is the idea of living a lifetime in the chilling shadow of this hill of shoes.

The imagery of the last three lines is compact and evocative, sharply highlighting the contrasts between the children who were chosen to die and the narrator, who was 'chosen to grow old'. Even the line 'I caught this cold' rings with echoes of childhood and stern parental warnings to take care and wrap up warm. Clive makes his own fate a mirror image of the children's, with the obvious parallel for all the rest of us who weren't at Auschwitz and were, like him, chosen to live:

And I caught this cold
When I was chosen to grow old
In the shadow of a hill of little shoes

Clive was perfectly well aware of the German philosopher Theodor Adorno's famous assertion that there could be no poetry after Auschwitz.

'I understood it, but I didn't believe it,' he says. 'Poetry is a form of knowledge, not of therapy; and nothing that humans do can be beyond its reach.'

Clive felt he had a useful and original perspective to add, and he felt a compulsion to say what he had to say. He has always believed that what the poet has inside him must come out and he has held to this view doggedly and consistently. As recently as April 2016, he was talking about this issue in an interview with the BBC's James Naughtie.

'You should write only what you must write,' he advised any poets who were listening. 'Write what you have to. I write to celebrate still being here.'

From a technical point of view, 'A Hill of Little Shoes' is very unusual. The opening lines of each of the first two stanzas and the last verse have simple single-syllable rhymes, in a strict ABAB scheme. Elsewhere, though, the rhymes that occur seem almost random. 'They', 'away' and 'day' provide three rhymes in the last four lines of the first verse. In the fourth stanza, the third and fifth lines rhyme. In the fifth verse, it's lines one and three, followed by the unexpected triple rhyme – 'bed', 'led' and 'instead' – that links the last three lines.

Rhyming is often used to provide a framework, a shape and creative discipline, in both songs and poetry. Here its function is different. The words read well as poetry on the page, but it is the occasional rhyme that helps to make 'A Hill of Little Shoes' a song lyric rather than a poem, reminding the listener that the sound is important, as well as the content of the lines.

For Pete, finding the right music for this extraordinary lyric was a considerable challenge. The easy option would have been to go for a poetry-and-jazz setting, without trying to impose a melody on these loosely-structured verses. Instead, he wrote a poignant tune that is among his very best, attaching it firmly to the rhymed parts of the first, second and last verses, and then developing ideas derived from its harmonies to support the more free-form stanzas in the middle of the song.

'Pete knew what was needed – monumentality, but with a legato line,' says Clive.

That shapely legato melody line, the proof that Pete had succeeded in turning the words into a real song, led to one of the rare covers of an Atkin/James composition. In 2010, the Northern folk trio Coope, Boyes and Simpson recorded an excellent three-part harmony version on their album *As If*, a track described by the *Guardian*'s Robin Denselow as 'a sturdy reworking of Clive James and Pete Atkin's pained and powerful "A Hill of Little Shoes"'.

Pete vividly recalls how the song came into being.

'My first encounter with "A Hill of Little Shoes" was over a Japanese lunch with Clive when we met to talk about the show we were going to do at Buxton Opera House in 1998,' he says. 'This was at a time when we'd seen each other only very rarely for several years, at the peak of my BBC involvement and Clive's involvement in TV. He "sang" it for me, using a repeated melodic phrase, and said he wanted to perform it at Buxton. We did it there and I accompanied his vocals with a very simple single minor chord figure throughout. But he also said he wasn't yet ready to hand the song over to me.'

Pete could feel the force of the lyric immediately and was eager to work on the song as soon as he was given the go-ahead. He began exploring some ideas, but it was nearly two years before Clive was happy to let him loose on it.

When he finally got the green light, he was determined not to blunt the impact of the lyrics by producing an ordinary melody-plus-chords song with a conventional rhythm and a predictable harmonic setting dictated by a familiar chord sequence.

'The motif I kept coming back to was the opening one, the phrase that acts as the intro, that stripped-down D minor thing. As usual, I followed where the words took me, leading me by different routes back to the opening idea. And that is how it grew, with several corner-turn moments along the way – like switching the tune to D major when it gets to "If you could find a pair".

'The hardest thing was deciding where to go musically with the line "They were like you in the same year". The focus changes a bit there, but I knew it couldn't be a standard middle-eight thing. I decided to take the tune emphatically back to D, but to put it harmonically somewhere else. So I took the tune up, knowing that I'd want to find a way to bring it back down for "another room instead".'

Both Clive and Pete have always believed the technical challenges of writing a special sort of song are the flint that strikes the creative spark. They like taking conventional forms and adapting them, sub-verting expectations and taking chances, setting themselves problems and finding new solutions that work in their own terms. Playing safe has never appealed to them.

'I remember, when I was very young, going to see the veteran jazz clarinettist Pee Wee Russell,' says Pete. 'He was amazing. You'd see an idea come into his head when he was playing a solo and he'd just go for it. Often it worked brilliantly. But sometimes he couldn't make the idea come together and he'd have to give up on it. When it fell apart, he'd just grin and shout "Bang!", out of the side of his mouth, while he was still playing. And he'd go right on to the next thing. I loved the danger and excitement and risk of going to the edge like that.'

In 'A Hill of Little Shoes', Clive and Pete showed that they could make the high-risk approach work triumphantly. It's a million miles from their early songs – the studied melancholy of 'Laughing Boy', the playfully romantic ingenuity of 'Have You Got a Biro I Can Borrow?' or the cheery flippancy of 'Practical Man' and 'Wristwatch for a Drummer'. But it proves, beyond doubt, that they have the skill and ambition to take their approach to popular songwriting to places we never thought it could visit, and to bring their audiences along with them on the journey into the darkness.

A Hill of Little Shoes

WORDS BY CLIVE JAMES, MUSIC BY PETE ATKIN

I live in the shadow of a hill,

A hill of little shoes.

I love, but I shiver with a chill,

A chill I never lose.

I live, I love, but where are they?

Where are their lives, their loves?

All blown away.

And every little shoe's a foot

That never grew another day

If you could find a pair

And put them on the floor,

Make a mark in the air

Like the marks beside your door

When you were growing,

You'd see how tall they were.

And the buckles and the laces

They could do up on their own,

Or almost could,

With their tongue tips barely showing,

Tell you how small they were

And then you think of little faces

Looking fearfully alone

And how they stood

In their bare feet, being tall for the last time,

Just to be good.

And that was all they were

They were like you in the same year.

But you grew up.

They were scarcely even here,

Before they suddenly weren't there.

And while you got dressed for bed,

They did the same, but they were led

Into another room instead

I live in the shadow of a hill,

A hill of little shoes.

I love, but I shiver with a chill,

A chill I never lose.

And I caught this cold

When I was chosen to grow old

In the shadow of a hill of little shoes

23

Perfect Moments

As the big Toyota SUV burns up the miles down a long straight road, the man with his head full of music hums silently to himself, under his breath. He's in his late fifties. The music's the usual random selection. 'I Got Rhythm'. 'California Dreaming'. Duke Ellington. 'Wonderwall'. A bit of Debussy. 'On the Road Again'.

'Spalding?' mutters his companion.

'Yeah. Not feeling too good myself,' he replies. 'We can stop for a cup of tea soon, if you like.'

While Pete drives, Clive is hunched in the seat to his left, working. He's got a small book and a notepad on his knee and he's translating Dante. This guy can work anywhere. It's a habit he's developed over the years of taking on too much and living with constant deadlines. He's learnt to use the hours in airports, to write poetry during the interminable delays in filming while shots are set up, to compose essays or translate Italian or read Russian classics in the car while the miles reel by.

'Don't say anything to Prue about this just yet,' he says. Clive's wife, Dr Prue Shaw, has been one of the country's leading experts on early Italian literature for several decades. 'I don't want her to know I'm doing Dante until I see how it's going.'

This is the rock 'n' roll life all right. They're on the road for a series of twenty gigs in just over a month, criss-crossing the country to play at theatres and universities, revelling in the enthusiastic reception they're getting from audiences young and old, fending off the over-attentive fans and enjoying just being together. They're too old to do it properly and trash their hotel rooms in the time-honoured tradition, though – and anyway, there's not much to trash. Mostly it's the spartan comforts of the Travelodge chain, with the odd night of relative luxury in a Premier Inn. But that's not a problem. Clive likes Travelodges.

'He's always said you don't need anything more than a decent bed, a clean shower and a desk to work on,' Pete recalls. 'Clive would walk into some anonymous budget hotel room, look at the bare surroundings and grin. "I could sit here for a month and write a book," he'd say. "It's got everything I want."

'When we toured in Australia and Hong Kong, we'd be playing in 2000-seater halls and being ferried round in a chauffeur-driven Lexus. It was first class all the way and we stayed in the top hotels, waited on hand and foot. Clive enjoys the finer things in life as much as the next man, but he was just as happy in a Travelodge.'

Back in the mid-Seventies, when Pete and Clive were on tour together to promote the *Live Libel* album, life was not so comfortable. The gigs were mainly in universities, accommodation was generally in dismal little B&Bs with nylon sheets, 40 watt lightbulbs and fussy landladies, and the lack of motorways (no M25, M11 or M60) made road trips long and slow. Clive was still not well known and he hadn't written a bestselling book. (*Unreliable Memoirs* was published in 1980 and provided the core of Clive's on-stage material when he and Pete went back on the road in the new millennium.) His contribution to the duo's performances mainly consisted of long, detailed and mostly funny introductions to the songs – and a little help with the singing.

He'd sing alternate verses of 'Laughing Boy', intone 'Why?' in his best gravel-voiced Telly Savalas drawl and sing along lustily with Pete on a couple of tuneful duets specially written for these shows. The set would end with one of these, 'Together At Last', which featured the most spectacular enjambement ever, stretching from the end of the middle eight right over and into the first line of the third verse. As this song is unlikely to be reprinted anywhere else, ever, under any circumstances and possibly for good artistic reasons, I will give you a couple of samples here. First, the enjambement. This is actually a fine example of the technique at its best. The line that leads up to it ('But when we team up we are two-') makes perfect sense in its own right. It is only when the next line begins that the audience realises, with a start, that the turn has come in mid-word, as the new verse begins with '-gether'.

For I, on my own, am but one man alone
And I know that the same goes for you.
But when we team up we are two-

-Gether at last,
Hearts that beat as one.
Swift and Stella, Perry and Della,
Dombey and Son

Writing like that brings tears to the eyes. And not only for those of us with fond and nostalgic memories of Flanders and Swann, who were apt to pull the same sort of bravura stunts. It's funny, of course. Audiences love to be surprised. But it takes a lot of skill to make a trick like that work. And the exultant rhyming of the last verse is also flamboyantly virtuoso stuff.

> Together at last,
> Boldly we move on.
> Ike and Tina, Frederick and Nina,
> Pope and Dryden, Mozart and Haydn,
> Clyde and Bonnie, Ronnie and Ronnie,
> Yoko and John
> Yoko and John?
> Yoko and John,
> Travelling on

How do you follow a closing number like that? Well, obviously, given enough applause to justify an encore, with another comic duet in a similar vein. 'There's No Truth in the Rumours (We're Just Friends)' is also in danger of being swept aside by the rush of history (and possibly condemned for what might be seen as a hint of homophobia), but it, too, has some lovely flourishes. 'Not that / We've anything of course / Against that special breed of lad / Or lass / Or cat or dog or horse / Whatever makes you feel good / Can't be bad' is essentially libertarian, surely, rather than anti-gay. The third verse begins with a flagrant bit of solmisation ('Do-re-mi-fa- / So here / Is where we must bow out') and the second bridge is a fine and ingenious piece of writing, with an unusual AABCCBB rhyme scheme, as used at various times by Pushkin and Byron.

> You think that we protest too much?
> We shiver at each other's touch?
> Perhaps we're repressing a deep need
> Did Sappho, Michelangelo
> And Proust know something we don't know,
> Along with Jean Cocteau and Andre Gide?
> And what about the Venerable Bede?

If the audience still had no homes to go to, Clive would lead into a final encore, an extraordinary rendition of Arthur 'Big Boy' Crudup's greatest hit, 'That's All Right (Mama)', as sung by Elvis Presley.

Pete's view of Clive's singing has always been tolerantly respectful.

'He can hold a tune all right,' he says, 'though his range is ever so slightly narrower than Ringo Starr's. His limitations as a singer are more to do with getting the timing. He always wants to come in too early. Clive's got a fabulous sense of rhythm when he's writing words, but physically he doesn't find it so easy. As he always says, he's the only person around who can't drum his fingers on a table and make the sound of a galloping horse. He can't do it. He just can't get the rhythm right.'

When Pete was able to get the mike to himself, one of the songs that went down best on tour – both in the 1970s and the 2000s – was a number that had appeared on *The Road of Silk*, 'Perfect

Moments'. It's a fine song in itself, but Pete found a particularly successful way of introducing it to audiences. He'd chat about the process of writing pop songs and about how he had tried to write a song using a ridiculously over-familiar and overused chord sequence that had been the basis of many great hits. He'd illustrate this with a long intro made up of two-bar snatches of some of the hundreds of well-known songs that use the C, Am, F, G7 chord progression – ranging from 'All I Have to Do Is Dream', 'Teenager in Love' and 'Take Good Care of My Baby' to Lennon/McCartney's 'Do You Want to Know a Secret?', the national anthem and 'Waltzing Matilda'. He'd then go into 'Perfect Moments', with its initial C and Am, and confound the expectations of those who didn't know the song with the next change, to a rather unconventional B flat.

'This is one where I started out with a conventional chord sequence,' says Pete. 'But as soon as the tune emerged, it took the song off somewhere else, because it demanded a different kind of harmony.'

The words Clive wrote for 'Perfect Moments' are very disciplined, divided strictly into four discrete sections. The first verse offers visual images of clean, geometrical perfection, the second pictures from the art galleries, the third icons (Charlie Chaplin and Charlie Parker) from popular culture. But it is the final verse that delivers the sucker punch.

Perfect moments should redeem the day.
Their teeming richness ought to be enough
To take the sting out of the other stuff.
A perfect bitch it doesn't work that way.

And Clive's right, of course. However many moments of joy and delight life hands us, it is always 'the other stuff' that dominates. Whatever sights we've seen and artistry we've enjoyed, it only takes a single bit of bad luck or bad news to ruin the day. We've been set up by the poetic prettiness of what comes before and we're not expecting the brutal force of the phrase 'perfect bitch'. It hits us out of the blue, deftly demonstrating exactly what the lyric as a whole has been saying. The impact is startling – so abrupt and deflating that we need the last line to be repeated, so we know we've heard it right.

'Perfect Moments' is one of a clutch of Atkin/James songs that carefully manipulate the audience into position to be socked on the jaw by a sudden twist in the last verse. 'The Hypertension Kid' catches us completely by surprise when the figure the narrator has been talking to melts into the mirror. Cottonmouth turns edgeways on and disappears like a razor blade seen from the side. 'Search and Destroy' tells its story of the heavyhanded suppression of an insurgent group in deceptively modern military slang, before rocking us back on our heels with the key lines ('The faithful talk some wishful-thinking cock / About a spook who rolls away the rock / At which point Golden Boy walks out alive') that reveal the biblical context.

All these songs depend on careful writing that creates a situation in which we let our guard down and leave ourselves open to an un-expected ending. On stage, the sheer surprise is almost guaranteed to get a positive reaction from any audience. But it is a sign of the quality of Clive's lyrics that, even when you've heard it dozens of times on the record and you know exactly what's coming, a song like 'Perfect Moments' can still put its point across.

Perfect Moments

WORDS BY CLIVE JAMES, MUSIC BY PETE ATKIN

Perfect moments have a clean design,
Scoring edges that arrest the flow.
Skis cut diamonds in the plump of snow.
Times my life feels like a friend of mine

Perfect moments wear a single face,
Variations on each other's theme.
Renoir's mistresses in peach and cream,
Rembrandt's mother in a ruff of lace

Perfect moments bear a single name.
They're placed together, though they never meet.
Charlie Chaplin policing Easy Street,
Charlie Parker playing 'My Old Flame'

Perfect moments should redeem the day.
Their teeming richness ought to be enough
To take the sting out of the other stuff.
A perfect bitch it doesn't work that way.
A perfect bitch it doesn't work that way

24

Taking Stock

For most of the last forty years, the six Pete Atkin albums from the 1970s – *Beware of the Beautiful Stranger, Driving Through Mythical America, A King at Nightfall, The Road of Silk, Secret Drinker* and *Live Libel* – have been out of print. There have been several reissues, but the companies involved have gone out of business or been taken over and the albums have disappeared again. People who knew where to look could hear the 73 songs from these classic LPs on Smash Flops, the Pete Atkin website, at www.peteatkin.com, but they couldn't go out and buy them and play them to their friends, so there were few new converts to the cause.

When the coming of the internet led to the formation of the Midnight Voices forum and fan group and the setting-up of the website, rekindling Pete's performing career, he quickly decided that he needed to take the fate of the newer Atkin/James material into his own hands. By making and distributing his own albums, pressing a couple of thousand at a time and going back with re-orders as stocks started to run low, he could make the online world work for him, act independently of the music industry's whims and accountants and ensure that any new album was always available.

Hillside Records was set up, operating from Pete's home in Bristol, and Pete began planning a new double album that would bring the fans up to date. In 2001, *The Lakeside Sessions, Vol 1: History and Geography* and *Vol 2: A Dream of Fair Women*, became the first Hillside Records release. It introduced 28 previously unheard songs, including all the tracks that had been planned (and even demoed) for the seventh 1970s album, which was never made. The production standards weren't lavish, but songs like 'Canoe', 'Search and Destroy', 'History and Geography' and Pete's own version of 'The Magic Wasn't There' gave the frustrated fans plenty to get their teeth into and the album sold well enough to encourage Pete to invest more time and money in the next Hillside project.

Winter Spring, which came out in 2003, brought ten new compositions and marked the first fruits of the renewed James/Atkin collaboration. It featured songs like 'Dancing Master', 'An Empty Table' and Clive's own favourite song.

'I'd be quite content to be remembered for a single lyric, "Winter Spring",' he told me recently, 'and I'm infinitely pleased that it's fitted so neatly to one of Pete's loveliest melodies.'

The most extraordinary achievement, though, was the haunting 'A Hill of Little Shoes', Clive's highly personal perspective on the tragedy of the children of the Auschwitz death camp.

After a couple of successful British tours in the early 2000s, Pete and Clive travelled further afield for the first time, playing fourteen big concerts at major venues in Australia (more than two thousand Sydneysiders packed the opulent State Theatre to see them) and two shows in Hong Kong. The mixed programme of songs and speech, with Pete playing a dozen numbers and Clive chatting with the audience and reading poems and passages from his memoirs, made for a remarkable evening.

'I can still remember Sydney. There were people laughing so much they were literally gasping for breath when Clive was reading the sequence from *Unreliable Memoirs* about the Dunny Man who used to come to empty the toilets when he was a kid,' says Pete. 'There were people in pain. But it's all in the timing, the pauses, the pacing of the delivery. You look at what he was reading on the page and it doesn't seem that funny. He doesn't do jokes at all. He just writes in a way that draws people into the situation and leaves them helpless with pleasure.'

There was a good quality recording of one of the other shows, in Perth, and this was released as a double CD, *Live in Australia*, giving enthusiasts their first chance to hear how Pete's versions of old favourites like 'Perfect Moments' and 'Thirty Year Man' had been changed and refined over the decades.

Pete had now been playing these songs and many others from the 1970s for thirty years, on and off. He was a better singer, more assured and confident in his timing and his ability to work a song. He knew he could deliver better performances, and there were some songs, such as 'Master of the Revels', 'Touch Has a Memory' and 'The Hypertension Kid' that had undergone quite radical changes of approach. So the idea gradually emerged that he should produce an Atkin's Greatest Hits of the Seventies album, which would give him a chance to revisit the old songs and also make sure that there would always be versions of them available for fans old and new.

The immediate stimulus for *Midnight Voices – The Clive James/Pete Atkin Songbook, Vol 1* was an invitation to sing at a disaster relief charity concert at St Georges, Bristol, in early 2007. Pete got together with a remarkably clever and sympathetic pianist, Simon Wallace, Mark Hodgson on bass and Roy Dodds on drums to form a band for the occasion. The rehearsals went well, and Pete soon realised something important was taking shape.

'As soon as we started working together, I began to get a new perspective on the songs,' he says. 'I wasn't necessarily trying to replace the older versions, but there were enough differences – a shift in tempo here, a change of rhythm there – to justify having another go at them.'

The approach to recording was different, too. Pete is an effective and imaginative pianist, but his technique is, as he says, 'functional, self-taught – I mostly just jab at the chords with the left hand and play the melody with my right'. With Simon Wallace taking over the piano, and adding a wealth of new ideas and harmonies, Pete was free to sing without playing at the same time. That wasn't something he'd ever tried, and it made a huge difference.

'I hardly play on the album at all,' he says. 'Apart from "Beware of the Beautiful Stranger", I hardly touch the guitar – and the piano is all Simon. It was a shock to me to discover how much better I could sing if I wasn't playing. I hadn't known that before.'

The fifteen tracks on Midnight Voices are generally more relaxed than the earlier versions of the same songs, with piano, rather than guitar, as the dominant instrument. The difference is particularly apparent on 'The Faded Mansion on the Hill', which had been one of the most impressive and powerful tracks on *Driving Through Mythical America*, the most 'electric' of the early albums.

'Faded Mansion' has everything. There's fine social observation in the lyrics ('When you see the litter of their lives, / The stupid children, bitter wives') and a sharp political awareness ('The beach the poor men never reach, / The shore the rich men never leave'), while the music consists of four superb and beautifully complementary tunes. The setting – it could be California or the millionaires' playground of the Hamptons, though, in fact, it was Sydney that Clive had in mind – is evoked with painterly skill, and even the distant sounds of 'shouts and falling sails', giving way to the stillness of the night, are brought to our attention. The song is rich, mysterious and unfathomable, opening out into a glorious union of words and music in the heavily-disguised 12-bar blues of the verse section.

> Between the headlands, to the sea, the fleeing yachts of summer go,
> White as a sheet and faster than the driven snow.
> Like dolphins riding high and giant seabirds flying low

This is arguably one of Pete's finest moments, an unexpected key change followed by a gorgeous, wistful melody that stops you in your tracks on first hearing and does it all over again whenever you come back to it.

'It's a wonderful piece of writing on Clive's part,' says Pete. 'I think it's an extraordinary song, full of depth and resonance. I can't say I've ever really got to the bottom of it, even now, but I'm still very proud of what I did with it.'

'Faded Mansion' worked well on the original album. On *Midnight Voices* it gains new poise and depth that make it a masterpiece. I had always thought it was one of those songs that could only be done by Pete, but this version makes it unexpectedly clear that it could be covered by any other artist with the ambition to take it on and make it his or her own.

It seems wrong to single out particular favourites from an album that doesn't have a dull track. The song about guitars and guitarists, 'Thief in the Night', comes up fresh as a daisy, with the surprising twist that there is now no guitar at all on the track (though there is a bamboo shakuhachi flute). 'The Hypertension Kid' has lost its shrill edge, and is all the better for it. 'The Flowers and the Wine' – the song Val Doonican covered – is just a perfect little gem about the end of love, still waiting for the right singer to make it a hit.

But the one track that demands to be mentioned is 'Thirty Year Man', the song the two young songwriters wrote forty-five years ago about the talented but jaded musician who had spent three decades in the business without achieving his due recognition.

The hero of the song is a nightclub pianist, part of the unsung quartet that sits in the shadows while the girl singer takes all the applause. We get a vivid picture of what the place is like when it's full, but the actual setting is the empty club some hours before the show. The man is there alone in the gloom, with only the darkened and empty tables and 'the covered-up drums and the microphone cables' for company, his piano glistening 'like the rail at the end of the nave' or 'like bones at the end of a cave'. He knows he's got talent, but he's missed the boat. He's reached middle age, but fame and freedom have passed him by and the nearest he comes to recognition is to be caught occasionally in the edge of the spotlight: 'And it's my bent-over back she's standing near.'

The subject matter plays to Clive's strongest suit, rueful melancholy. There's a weary, resigned fatalism about the man's attitude, doubly painful because he still has a romantic attachment to his art. When he plays on stage, no-one notices him, yet when he's on his own he still does what a musician must and plays 'a few things' for his own pleasure, quietly rejoicing in the freedom to choose his own music and assert his own identity for a precious hour before the evening's work starts.

As Clive wrote in his sleeve notes to the 2009 reissue of *A King at Nightfall*, 'the sense of loss was already there' in many of the Atkin/James songs of the 1970s.

'We put a lot of premature melancholy into our early work. God, it was fun, though, and I like to think that even the Thirty Year Man has some great times to look back on.'

Pete's music frames and reinforces the words with deft and gently ironic precision. Having a keyboard player as the hero enables the piano part to be an element in the story, as well as commenting on it, and the result is a series of delightful moments as Simon Wallace switches across a range of more or less hackneyed piano styles. The lazy, rolling swing that propels the chorus contrasts with the introspective backing that underpins the man's musings and the more imaginative tinklings at the end, when the hero is playing, briefly, for himself.

There is something very satisfying about the merging of words and music in this song, about the quiet precision with which the lyrics and the notes match up with the underlying theme. It sounds true and familiar, like a song you've heard before, even if you haven't. Clive and Pete's ambition was always to produce modern songs in the old tradition of the Great American Songbook, where creativity and craftsmanship came together to make seamless and apparently effortless works of genius. 'Thirty Year Man' may not be Gershwin or Porter, but it gets pretty close.

Thirty Year Man

WORDS BY CLIVE JAMES, MUSIC BY PETE ATKIN

Nobody here yet.
From the spotlight that will ring her not a glimmer.
Not a finger on its squeaky dimmer.
I play piano in a jazz quartet
That works here late with a young girl singer

And along from the darkened and empty tables,
By the covered-up drums and the microphone cables,
At the end of the room, the piano glistens,
Like the rail at the end of the nave

Thirty years in the racket,
A brindled crew cut and a silk-lined jacket.
And it isn't my hands that fill this place.
It's a kid's voice still reaching into space.
It's her they're driving down to hear
And it's my bent-over back she's standing near

Nobody talks yet.

From the glasses that will touch soon not a tinkle.

Not a paper napkin shows a wrinkle.

I play piano in a jazz quartet

That backs a winner while the big notes crinkle

And along from the darkened and empty tables,

By the covered-up drums and the microphone cables,

At the end of the room, the piano glistens,

Like the rail at the end of the nave.

And I play a few things, while no-one listens

Thirty years in the racket,

A brindled crew cut and a silk-lined jacket.

And it isn't my name that brings them in.

It's a little girl just starting to begin.

It's her they're piling in to see

And I'd kill that kid, if she wasn't killing me

Nobody moves yet.

From the tables near the bandstand not a rustle.

Not a loudmouth even moves a muscle.

I play piano in a jazz quartet

That backs a giver while the takers hustle

And along from the darkened and empty tables,

By the covered-up drums and the microphone cables,

At the end of the room, the piano glistens,
Like bones at the end of a cave.
And I play a few things, while no-one listens.
For an hour alone spells freedom to the slave

25

Double Six

For more than five years, Clive James has been fighting a slow, gruelling battle against leukaemia, emphysema and kidney failure – 'the lot', as he calls it. He has been kept alive by the extraordinary efforts of the doctors and nursing teams at Addenbrooke's Hospital in Cambridge and kept productive by his own restless energy and curiosity. A string of medical advances have helped buy him time, but he will not be lucky for ever.

'In my condition, you have to go on throwing a double six just to stay in the game,' he wrote recently.

Despite his poor health and ebbing stamina, Clive has made productive use of the extra time he has been given. He has finally completed and published the translation of Dante's *Divine Comedy* he was working on in the car when he and Pete were on the road to Spalding fourteen years ago. He has written a number of remarkable new poems – most notably 'Sentenced to Life' and 'Japanese Maple' – that have broken through to reach and move millions who don't normally read poetry. He has seen his recent book of literary essays, *Latest Readings*, and his *Poetry Notebook: 2006–2014* delight and inspire some critics and infuriate others – par for the course and just what he would have wanted. In April 2016, his mighty 580-page *Collected Poems* was published, alongside his *Gate of Lilacs: A Verse Commentary on Proust*, probably one of the most eccentric literary endeavours of the year.

For a man whose strength is almost gone, Clive has remained extraordinarily busy and engaged. He has continued writing for the *Guardian* and others and he still feels the impulse to condense his deeply personal insights and ideas into poetry. 'I am now going to read myself in today's *TLS*, before I get back to read more about myself in Ian's draft chapters, and then get on with expressing myself in a new poem,' he wrote in a recent email to Pete. 'It saves me from contemplating my navel.'

The Atkin/James partnership is unlikely to produce any more new songs. But there are signs, even in the most recent poems, of how ideas and phrases have passed backwards and forwards between the two forms. When Clive writes, in a poem called 'Landfall', 'I am here now, who was hardly even there', we recognise the idea that first saw the light of day in 'A Hill of Little Shoes'. In the song, it was the children of Auschwitz who were 'scarcely even here, / before they suddenly weren't there'. Now it is Clive, paradoxically 'restored by my decline', who is more here than he's ever been.

In the last five years, Clive has consolidated his position as a real, substantial poet and an important voice of his generation. Even as I write that, though, I'm aware it's a cliché. The true voice of Clive's generation and mine is the voice of the singer, not the poet. It's Lennon, not Larkin. We were the first generation who could choose what we listened to and where we listened to it, and the generations that have followed have moved on to acquire the same access to video material, leaving us behind in our audio world, our world of music and words. It still surprises me that the songs Clive and Pete wrote never became part of that mainstream, but they will always be there for those who are interested in tracking them down, if only via the website at www.peteatkin.com.

In January 2016, just after we had agreed that this book should be written, Pete Atkin went out for a walk near his home in Bristol and was hit by a bus. He suffered terrible injuries – smashed eye sockets, five fractures to the jaw, a bleed on the brain and severe damage to his left wrist – and was in a medically-induced coma for four days. After five weeks in hospital, he came home and began a long and surprisingly successful period of recovery, in the care of his loving and protective American wife, Mary. The emergency surgery that saved his life by reducing the pressure on his brain has left him with no sight in his right eye, but his voice is still clear and strong, his wrist is on the mend and he is optimistic about the future.

'In terms of scarring or permanent damage, I scarcely look as if anything much has happened to me at all,' he says. 'There's no reason why I can't start performing again – and fairly soon, I hope.'

The classic Pete Atkin albums of the Seventies are currently un-available. The rights to the recordings have been passed from hand to hand and become caught up in company mergers and bankruptcies, and no-one knows, at this point, whether they will ever be reissued again. But Pete's excellent remakes of fifteen of the key tracks are available on his 2007 album, *Midnight Voices*, and the last CD of new songs, *The Colours of the Night*, released in 2015, is currently selling faster than anything else he's done since the early days.

The final track on *The Colours of the Night* is a fitting epilogue to nearly fifty years of Atkin/James collaboration. It's called 'Me to Thank', and this time it's personal (one Amazon reviewer described the song as being 'Like "My Way" – only true'). Unlike the other tracks on the album, made with a wonderful band featuring the return of Chris Spedding on guitar and the superbly supportive Simon Wallace on piano, this track just has Pete, on his own, singing and playing a simple, loose piano accompaniment. It's not the most commercial song on the album – 'The Way You Are With Me', 'We Will Love Again' and the doo-wop pop of 'Slow Down for Me' are far more likely to be picked up and covered by other singers – but it is the most intimate and heartfelt. The poignant lyrics are disciplined by the demands of a strict rhyme scheme and there are only occasional flashes of Clive's moth-to-the-flame compulsion to go for the big line ('I've got to where it's hard to find the sleep so you can dream / I've got to wear a diving suit to find my self-esteem').

'I think that song is a miracle of simplicity,' says Pete. 'There are no party tricks, but it's one of the cleverest, most tightly crafted lyrics Clive has ever written. It's taken a lifetime of experiment and practice to achieve that simplicity, that natural, spoken-word quality.

'When you're young and innocent and you know nothing, simplicity may well come naturally. It gets harder to achieve when you know a bit. Clive knows a lot, but he can do it.'

Clive and Pete have always been fond of the free-form, out-of-tempo introductory verses that came before the main body of the song in so many of the great Tin Pan Alley classics. They used the technique themselves in songs like 'Senior Citizens'. Here, though, we have what's effectively an out-of-tempo preamble with no song to follow. There's no post-amble, no catchy in-tempo chorus, just a quiet, downbeat ending. And the lack of tempo means the song relies heavily on the innocent sophistication of the rhyming to carry it along and give it shape.

'When people talk about clever rhyming, they're usually thinking about outrageous, inventive, tricksy rhymes,' says Pete. 'And there's never been anyone to touch Clive for that. But the sheer skill of his rhyming here trumps any kind of clever-cleverness.'

Clive can't help being clever, though, and delighting in his craft. In the bridge passage, for example, the shifting rhythm and cunning rhymes create an effect that adds something beyond the meaning of the words.

> I've got me to thank
> I don't blame you even slightly.
> I should have made my sorrow brightly lit,
> And put it lightly.
> Not the same complaint twice nightly,
> Holding on to you too tightly

This is not just poetry. It's made for the voice, not for the page. But it's not quite what we're used to in a song, either. Perhaps that is what's kept Clive and Pete's creations out of the spotlight for all these years. From time to time they've invented something that sits between song and poetry and doesn't fit in, except on its own terms. There are songs of theirs that should have been left on the page, as poetry, and at least a dozen – from 'The Magic Wasn't There', 'The Flowers and the Wine' and 'Thirty Year Man' to 'Faded Mansion on the Hill', 'Dancing Master' and 'The Way You Are With Me' – that are triumphantly and emphatically successful pop songs, in a wide variety of genres.

With 'Me to Thank', Clive and Pete are effectively saying goodbye to half a century of working together. The valediction is there in Clive's words and, less explicitly, in the last few jazz-tinged phrases of Pete's piano. It is the end. But something of their partnership will go on into the future. 'Ars longa, vita brevis', as Hippocrates once said (though it won't have sounded quite like that, as he spoke Greek, rather than Latin). The 'art' he referred to was actually 'craft' or 'technique' (as in the Art of War or the Art of Seduction), rather than 'art' as in painting, music and literature. Either way – or both – life is short but the other thing lives on.

Me to Thank

WORDS BY CLIVE JAMES, MUSIC BY PETE ATKIN

I've got to where it's hard to find the tears so you can weep.
I've got to where the step up to the carpet is too steep.
I've got to where, apart from air,
There's nothing in the tank.
And I like to think that I had time to thank.
But I've got me to thank.
I've got me to thank

I've got me to thank.

I should have spoken to you clearly,

And now the chance is nearly

Gone, and I pay dearly

I've got me to thank

I don't blame you even slightly.

I should have made my sorrow brightly lit,

And put it lightly.

Not the same complaint twice nightly,

Holding on to you too tightly

I've got to where it's hard to find the sleep so you can dream.

I've got to wear a diving suit to find my self-esteem.

I've got to where I hardly care

There's nothing in the bank.

And I'd like to think that I had time to think of who or what to

thank.

But when I do, I draw a blank.

I've got me to thank.

I've got me to thank

26

The Thinking Man's Hagiography

You may have noticed by now that I am very keen on the songs Pete Atkin and Clive James wrote together over the years. Not all of the songs, of course, and not all the parts of the songs I like. But that's not enough to stop my enthusiasm in its tracks. Only Shakespeare can write like Shakespeare all the time. But that doesn't stop other poets, like John Donne, for instance, from giving us huge amounts of pleasure.

Donne is a perfect example. On his day, he could write like Shakespeare. Seen in the right light, Donne's most famous phrases, 'No man is an island' and 'for whom the bell tolls', could easily be mistaken for Shakespeare, and often are. And his delight in language, his love of irony and paradox and his fondness for bold puns, outrageous conceits and metaphors and natural colloquial speech rhythms make him the most readable and attractive of the Bard's poetic contemporaries. He wrote about love and sex, rogues and fools, sickness and death, grief and exile, fleas and philosophy, and he did it with an exuberant energy that frequently annoyed the straitlaced critics of his own and later generations. When Samuel Johnson coined the term 'metaphysical poets' to describe Donne and contemporaries like

Marvell, Herbert and Vaughan, it wasn't meant as a compliment. As far as Johnson was concerned, they were all too fond of showing off and indulging in intellectual acrobatics. 'The metaphysical poets were men of learning, and, to show their learning was their whole endeavour,' he wrote, adding that they typically used 'heterogeneous ideas yoked by violence together'.

Worse, they were shameless about how this violent yoking was done. 'Nature and art are ransacked for illustrations, comparisons, and allusions,' moaned the good doctor. He was prepared to give Donne and the others credit for 'subtility', but claimed that, in the end, readers were 'seldom pleased'.

That wasn't true then, of course, and it isn't true now. People love this sort of stuff. And it is interesting to note that all these criticisms of Donne and his poetically boisterous peers are remarkably similar to the charges that have sometimes been levelled at Clive's poetry and song lyrics.

When Robert Burton, in the preface to *The Anatomy of Melancholy* (1621), accused Donne and the rest of them of 'neat composition, hyperboles, allegories' and other crimes like 'affectations of big words, fustian phrases, jingling termes, strong lines, that like Acaste's arrows caught fire as they flew', he meant it to hurt. But Donne survived the assault, and Clive's best lyrics are guilty of all the same grievous and life-enhancing sins.

Clive James has that same insatiable urge to amuse and entertain, to delight and startle. He wants to drag in ideas and allusions from every possible source. He does like to show off his learning, but he revels in the cadences of real speech, too. (Right at the beginning, in the title track of the very first album, *Beware of the Beautiful Stranger*, Clive comes up with several snatches of dialogue that could be straight out of *Eastenders*. 'The lady in question is known to me now, and I'd like to beware, but the problem is how?' says the man. 'That's your lot,' says Miss Lee, as she turns on the light, 'These earrings are hell and I'm through for the night.')

In fact, the comparison between Clive and John Donne is not at all farfetched. There was a new wave of enthusiasm for Donne in the Sixties, sparked by the publication of Helen Gardner's *Metaphysical Poets* collection in 1957, just a few years before the kid from Kogarah arrived in Cambridge. Metaphysical poetry was in the air (indeed, I'm hoping this chapter will partly compensate, a bit belatedly, for my own essay on the Metaphysical poets that I failed to hand in to my tutor at York University in 1969). Clive certainly knew and appreciated Donne then, and he even went on, much later, to write a thoughtful poem about him, 'Dream Me Some Happiness', which was included in *The Book of My Enemy: Collected Verse, 1958-2003*.

John Donne was incredibly sexy and vividly topical in his choice of imagery ('Licence my roving hands, and let them goe / Behind, before, above, between, below / Oh my America, my new found lande'). He could turn a beautifully seductive phrase ('If ever any beauty I did see / Which I desir'd, and got, 'twas but a dream of thee'). And he famously stretched the boundaries of metaphor. Two lovers are mingled in the blood the flea has sucked from them ('Don't squash it,' he says, or words to that effect, 'It's us as well. Spare three lives in one flea. Oops, now look what you've done'). The lovers are a pair of compasses, the woman tracing the perimeter of the circle, while the man, staying

195

at the centre point, leans out towards her and waits expectantly for the other compass point's return ('And growes erect, as it comes home'). Donne loved offbeat ideas and clearly wrote for his own amusement, rejoicing in his own ingenuity and wordplay. He even used the obvious pun on his own name, writing tersely to his wife, Anne, after losing his job, 'John Donne, Anne Donne, Un-done.' Like Clive, he would rather try risking something spectacular, even if it might not come off, than settle for the conventional image or the routine phrase.

When Clive yokes together the Polynesian islanders in their canoe and the three astronauts on Apollo 13, he is plucking an extraordinary and unlooked-for parallel out of his subconscious. When he describes a brutal crackdown on a small group of religiously-motivated insurgents in the Middle East and abruptly twists this 21st-century situation to link it with the fate of Jesus and his disciples, the sheer audacity of the comparison takes your breath away, jolting your perspective and challenging a lot of cosy assumptions. When he cuts from a seedy London pub to the pleasure palaces of Versailles, in 'Payday Evening', the effect is positively cinematic, an unexpected juxtaposition that adds a new dimension to the song.

At their best, Clive's lyrics, like his poems, are full of the same racy, reckless ambition we see in John Donne. If his leaps of imagination sometimes miss their mark or sound as if he's tried too hard, the beauty and power of his best work provide ample compensation for the occasional misfiring line.

When I asked Clive recently about his debt to the Metaphysicals, he agreed that studying Donne, both at Sydney University and later at Cambridge, had influenced his attitudes to poetry and lyric writing.

'But the main conscious influence was always Andrew Marvell,' he told me. 'Especially "The Definition of Love", which I can still recite from memory in its beautifully neat entirety.'

This is a poem I had almost forgotten, though it turns out that Pete, too, knows it by heart. It is based on the central image of two lovers as the poles of the world, thwarted by fate and destined by both geography and geometry to be apart for ever. 'As lines so loves oblique may well / Themselves in every angle greet / But ours so truly parallel, / Though infinite can never meet' the poet says. The verse doesn't have the crackling, rumbustious energy of Donne's best work, or even the ringing, sonorous lines that stand out in Marvell's own best-known poem, 'To His Coy Mistress' ('But at my back I always hear / Time's winged chariot hurrying near' and 'The grave's a fine and private place / But none I think do there embrace'). What it does have is a near-perfect balance and control, with effortlessly flexible speech rhythms within a tight rhyme scheme and a general air of polished craftsmanship. I can see why Clive admires it, but I still think his own work – both poetry and lyrics – would strike most people as much more obviously Donne-ish than Marvellian.

When it comes to the actual content of the lyrics, Clive is extremely scrupulous. Playing fast and loose with the facts is not his way. If there's a line that seems puzzling, you'll usually find that he is referring to something real and factually checkable. If 'Well, at last we pulled in and as straight as a three-sided knife / She got up and walked like a princess away from my life' (in 'Girl on the Train') seems to jar, it may help to know that a three-sided knife is actually a particularly narrow and vicious type of stiletto. If you're troubled by the reference in 'Payday Evening' to 'Pompadour's theatre in the stairs', it may help to know that Madame de Pompadour really did have a miniature theatre, decked out in blue and silver, installed in the well of the great Staircase of the Ambassadors at Versailles. Or it may just make you want to slap Clive for knowing too much and not keeping it to himself.

As the poet once said, nobody's perfect. And no-one, in any field, can get it absolutely right all the time. I was fourteen the day after 'Love Me Do' was released. I grew up and have lived my whole life in the shadow of the 300-odd songs recorded by the Beatles. My admiration for how they changed music and the world is unbounded. But, like anyone, I could easily reel off a list of the Beatles' Ten Worst Songs (all right, then: 'Mr Moonlight', 'Savoy Truffle', 'I'll Get You', 'Everybody's Got Something to Hide Except Me and My Monkey', 'All Together Now', 'Rocky Raccoon', 'Run For Your Life', nominated by Lennon as his own anti-favourite, the dirge-like 'Long, Long, Long', 'Don't Pass Me By' and, of course, 'Revolution #9'). The point is never how bad an artist's worst work is; it's how good the best can be.

When I started writing this book, Pete Atkin asked me what I was trying to do. 'It'll be a hagiography,' I said. 'I love so many of your songs. But it'll have to be a thinking man's hagiography, with a bit of provocation here and there and a sense of light and shade, or no-one will bother to read past the first page or two.' So that's what I have been aiming to achieve in this book. I've been painfully aware, over and over again, that readers of the hardback, rather than the ebook, will not have the luxury of being able to click straight through and hear the songs as they are reading about them. But virtually every song mentioned here can be heard on the Music Player section of Pete's quaintly old-fashioned website, at www.peteatkin.com, alongside a mass of radio recordings, demos, out-takes and interviews. It's important to hear these creations as songs, rather than reading them as lyrics on the page, if only to marvel at the challenges Pete has sometimes had to overcome to make them singable.

I don't expect anyone to share my enthusiasm for all these songs. But I can't imagine there'll be many people who will fail to find something to tickle their fancy among these neglected masterpieces. The fifty-year collaboration between Clive James and Pete Atkin has created a legacy that will always be worth exploring. These songs have already given me immense pleasure over many years, but I'm almost jealous of those who are discovering them now and have all that delight ahead of them.

Acknowledgements

My sincere thanks and appreciation go to Clive James and Pete Atkin, without whom – well, obviously, without whom there'd be nothing. No songs, no story, no book, no nothing. Apart from those views directly quoted from the two of them, Pete and Clive bear no responsibility whatever for the opinions expressed in this book, all of which are my own, or shamelessly stolen from the comments of people brighter than me.

I am indebted to Stephen Fry for his lucid, impassioned and poetic foreword. I love his reckless TS Eliot misquote: 'Here is no water, only rock and roll', and the wonderfully graphic image of the music wrapping around the words and the words wrapping around the music 'like Escher's drawing hands'. I know what writing costs writers. Even for someone of Stephen's flashing brilliance, putting together an essay of such scope and detail is no small task. I hugely appreciate the time, effort and craft he gave so freely.

Among those who have helped me enormously are Hayley Redmond, Stephen Birkill, whose enthusiasm and initiative led directly to the rebooting of Clive and Pete's songwriting career in the 1990s, Robin Bynoe, whose views (often at variance with my own, as the lawyers like to say) gave me a variety of new angles and insights into the strengths and subtleties of these remarkable songs, and the eagle-eyed Kate Penning, whose encouragement and critical reading of each draft chapter inspired several significant changes and spurred me on to finish what I'd started. My son, Nick, also turned out to be a shrewd critic and the source of several new ideas that have greatly enriched the book.

I am grateful, too, to Clare Christian and Heather Boisseau of RedDoor Publishing, for their support, suggestions, friendship and gently insistent professionalism. Steve Birkill (again) made many helpful comments and corrections and provided many of the photographs in the book, including his own superb shot of Pete and Clive together on stage at the High Wycombe concert in April 2002. I would also like to thank Seán Kelly for permission to use his picture of Pete playing at Walthamstow Folk Club in November 2015, Sophie Baker for the atmospheric shot of Pete at Morgan Studios during the sessions for *A King at Nightfall*, Christopher Parry for the historic photo of Pete's first-ever solo gig (at Sittingbourne FE College in 1969) and Gerald Smith for letting me include his shot of Pete and Clive both singing their hearts out in concert at Canterbury in 2005.

The delightfully prophetic photograph of a young and well-barbered Clive James hammering out material for the Sydney University magazine, using an enormous old typewriter and surrounded by a bevy of admirers, dates from early 1960 and was taken for the *Sydney Morning Herald*. This fine picture is copyright B Newberry/Fairfax Syndication and is used by permission.

Copyright Credits

My grateful thanks to Clive James, Pete Atkin and the music publishers involved – Bucks Music Group, Onward Music, Essex Music and Westminster Music – for permission to quote from and reprint the lyrics of these songs. Where no publisher is named for a particular song, copyright control remains directly in the hands of Pete Atkin and Clive James.

All I Ever Did
Composed by Pete Atkin
© Westminster Music Ltd, Suite 2.07, Plaza 535, King's Road, London, SW10 0SZ
International copyright secured. All rights reserved. Used by permission

All the Dead Were Strangers
Composed by Pete Atkin, lyrics by Clive James
© Onward Music Ltd, Roundhouse, London, NW1 8AW
Used with permission

Ballad of an Upstairs Window
Music and lyrics by Pete Atkin
© Bucks Music Group Ltd, Roundhouse, London, NW1 8AW
Used with permission

Be Careful When They Offer You the Moon
Composed by Pete Atkin, lyrics by Clive James
© Onward Music Ltd, Roundhouse, London, NW1 8AW
Used with permission

Beware of the Beautiful Stranger
Composed by Pete Atkin, lyrics by Clive James
© Onward Music Ltd, Roundhouse, London, NW1 8AW
Used with permission

Carnations on the Roof
Composed by Pete Atkin, lyrics by Clive James
© Bucks Music Group Ltd, Roundhouse, London, NW1 8AW
Used with permission

The Faded Mansion on the Hill
Composed by Pete Atkin, lyrics by Clive James
© Westminster Music Ltd, Suite 2.07, Plaza 535, King's Road, London,
SW10 0SZ
International copyright secured. All rights reserved. Used by permission

Girl on the Train
Composed by Pete Atkin, lyrics by Clive James
© Onward Music Ltd, Roundhouse, London, NW1 8AW
Used with permission

Have You Got a Biro I Can Borrow?
Composed by Pete Atkin, lyrics by Clive James
© Onward Music Ltd, Roundhouse, London, NW1 8AW
Used with permission

The Hypertension Kid
Composed by Pete Atkin, lyrics by Clive James
© Onward Music Ltd, Roundhouse, London, NW1 8AW
Used with permission

Laughing Boy
Composed by Pete Atkin, lyrics by Clive James
© Onward Music Ltd, Roundhouse, London, NW1 8AW
Used with permission

The Magic Wasn't There
Composed by Pete Atkin, lyrics by Clive James
© Westminster Music Ltd, Suite 2.07, Plaza 535, King's Road, London,
SW10 0SZ
International copyright secured. All rights reserved. Used by permission

The Paper Wing Song
Music and lyrics by Clive James
© Bucks Music Group Ltd, Roundhouse, London, NW1 8AW
Used with permission

Payday Evening
Composed by Pete Atkin, lyrics by Clive James
© Bucks Music Group Ltd, Roundhouse, London, NW1 8AW
Used with permission

Practical Man
Composed by Pete Atkin, lyrics by Clive James
© Onward Music Ltd, Roundhouse, London, NW1 8AW
Used with permission

Screen-Freak
Composed by Pete Atkin, lyrics by Clive James
© Westminster Music Ltd, Suite 2.07, Plaza 535, King's Road, London,
SW10 0SZ
International copyright secured. All rights reserved. Used by permission

Senior Citizens
Composed by Pete Atkin, lyrics by Clive James
© Bucks Music Group Ltd, Roundhouse, London, NW1 8AW
Used with permission

Sessionman's Blues
Composed by Pete Atkin, lyrics by Clive James
© Bucks Music Group Ltd, Roundhouse, London, NW1 8AW
Used with permission

Song for Rita
Composed by Pete Atkin, lyrics by Clive James
© Bucks Music Group Ltd, Roundhouse, London, NW1 8AW
Used with permission

Stranger in Town
Composed by Pete Atkin, lyrics by Clive James
© Bucks Music Group Ltd, Roundhouse, London, NW1 8AW
Used with permission

Thirty Year Man
Composed by Pete Atkin, lyrics by Clive James
© Westminster Music Ltd, Suite 2.07, Plaza 535, King's Road, London, SW10 0SZ
International copyright secured. All rights reserved. Used by permission

Touch Has a Memory
Composed by Pete Atkin, lyrics by Clive James
© Westminster Music Ltd, Suite 2.07, Plaza 535, King's Road, London, SW10 0SZ
International copyright secured. All rights reserved. Used by permission

Wristwatch for a Drummer
Composed by Pete Atkin, lyrics by Clive James
© Onward Music Ltd, Roundhouse, London, NW1 8AW
Used with permission

Index